Broadman Comments

July-September, 1990

on
THE INTERNATIONAL
BIBLE LESSONS
for
Christian Teaching

CONVENTION UNIFORM SERIES

Volume 45 Number 4

BROADMAN PRESS
NASHVILLE, TENNESSEE

This material was first published in
Broadman Comments, 1989–90

4215-80
ISBN: 0-8054-1580-7

Broadman Comments *is published quarterly by Broadman Press,
127 Ninth Avenue, North, Nashville, Tennessee 37234.
When ordered with other church literature, it sells for $3.50 per quarter.
Second-class postage paid at Nashville, Tennessee.*

ISSN 0068-2721

POSTMASTER: Send address change to *Broadman Comments*,
Customer Service Center, 127 Ninth Avenue, North
Nashville, Tennessee 37234

Dewey Decimal Classification 268.81
Printed in the United States of America

Contents

Wisdom As a Way of Life

Prophets, Priests, and Kings

Abbreviations and Translations

July 1

Get Wisdom at All Cost

Basic Passage: Proverbs 4

Focal Passage: Proverbs 4:1-13

Who were our teachers, the people who influenced our lives in youth so that today we give thanks for their instruction and example? This lesson invites us to look back and bear tribute to our benefactors. There is a recognizable chain of dependence so that teachers of today acknowledge themselves as the taught of yesterday, and the taught of today face the challenge to become the teachers of tomorrow. Each generation is answerable for the next. This is true in terms of citizenship and community relationships. The world of the twenty-first century, which is only ten years aways, will depend on the kind of people we are today and the measure in which we have fulfilled our obligations to the men and women of the future. As Christians, we are challenged not only to stand strong for good education, democratic principles, and law and order, but more importantly for those standards of behavior and belief that are the essence of the gospel. We have a legacy to leave in our Christian faith that can determine, more than anything else, what kind of future is ahead.

Study Aim: *To esteem scriptural wisdom (teaching) so highly* *that we will increasingly seek it for ourselves and share it with others*

STUDYING THE BIBLE

The earlier verses of Proverbs 4 contain strong echoes of the content of chapter 1. There are important differences, which we will bring out, but enough similarities to encourage the use of the entire chapter to bring its total message into service.

I. A Teacher's Memories (Prov. 4:1-4)

As already indicated, "ye children" are not the words of a parent but of a teacher comparing himself to a father (v. 1). He was not acting in place of, but filling the same role as, a parent. The assumption is that what the student had learned in the home is being reinforced by what he learns in school. We know little about schooling among the Hebrews, but the strong emphasis given to the instruction of children (Deut. 6:6-7; Josh. 4:21-22), and the compiling of the Book of Proverbs as a manual of instruction, provide reasons to believe that schools existed.

1 Hear, ye children, the instruction of a father, and attend to know understanding.

2 For I give you good doctrine, forsake ye not my law.

3 For I was my father's son, tender and only beloved in the sight of my mother.

4 He taught me also, and said unto me, Let thine heart retain my words: keep my commandments, and live.

The teacher recalls his own childhood and provides a beautiful picture of family life. He was an only child, "the only one in the sight of my mother" (RSV). Though much loved, he was not spoiled for when he was "tender," that is, very young, his father became his teacher. He urged the child to take his instruction to heart, as we still say. To the Hebrews, the heart was not so much the center of emotions as of intelligence and memory. By taking his father's counsel seriously the young child would get the best out of life. A constant emphasis in Proverbs is that right living brings its rewards, a truth not to be argued against although an explanation of the nature of these rewards is needed. Too many good people meet with misfortune for these rewards to be thought of in totally material terms.

II. The Love of Wisdom (Prov. 4:5-9)

Basing his words on his own experience, the teacher urges his pupils to "get wisdom." We must again remind ourselves that this does not mean to qualify in scholarship, or professional skills, or technology, but to learn how to live acceptably before God and toward others. The importance of this is brought out in verse 7, "with all thy getting get understanding," the meaning of which is, "whatever else you get, be sure you get wisdom." Solomon made this his priority in response to God's invitation, "Ask what I shall give thee." In his response, the king asked for "an understanding heart," a request that the Lord commended. Because Solomon had not asked for other desirable things, the Lord said, "Lo, I have given thee a wise and an understanding heart. . . . I have also given thee that which thou hast not asked, both riches, and honour: so that there shall not be any among the kings like unto thee all thy days" (1 Kings 3:5-14).

5 Get wisdom, get understanding: forget it not; neither decline from the words of my mouth.

6 Forsake her not, and she shall preserve thee: love her, and she shall keep thee.

7 Wisdom is the principal thing; therefore get wisdom: and with all thy getting get understanding.

8 Exalt her, and she shall promote thee: she shall bring thee to honour, when thou dost embrace her.

9 She shall give to thine head an ornament of grace: a crown of glory shall she deliver to thee.

Again, Wisdom is personified in terms of a highly desirable woman, perhaps a bride. She has so much to offer that nothing should be allowed to stand in the way of obtaining her. The idea of purchase is present. This was in accord with Eastern practice. Jacob gained Rachel as wife by paying her father Laban, with seven years of hard work, "and they seemed unto him but a few days, for the love he had to her" (Gen. 29:20). Jacob and Rachel shared an unusual love. A New Testament parallel is our Lord's parable of the pearl of great price (Matt. 13:45-46).

III. Rewards of the Wise (Prov. 4:10-13)

At this point begins a contrast between two ways, "the way of wisdom" (v. 11) and "the way of evil men" (v. 14). The teacher is still persuading his pupil, "my son," to accept the instruction offered. The consequence will be long life, a coveted prize in Hebrew thought, and still considered desirable. A safe walk as long as life lasts is also promised, "When you walk your step will not be hampered; and if you run, you will not stumble" (v. 12, RSV). Adherence to high moral and ethical principles is always a plus in life. Incidents and circumstances that cause trouble for other people can be successfully handled and overcome by those who, because of their faith in God, live clean lives and maintain good attitudes.

> **10 Hear, O my son, and receive my sayings; and the years of thy life shall be many.**
> **11 I have taught thee in the way of wisdom; I have led thee in right paths.**
> **12 When thou goest, thy steps shall not be straitened; and when thou runnest, thou shalt not stumble.**
> **13 Take fast hold of instruction; let her not go: keep her; for she is thy life.**

Presumably, the instruction given by this Old Testament teacher is assembled in the Book of Proverbs. As Christians, we need to realize that we have a superior manual for life in the New Testament. Some of its more important teaching is condensed into the Sermon on the Mount which touches on many of the themes discussed in Proverbs. Jesus spoke about the broad way "that leadeth to destruction," over against the narrow way "which leadeth unto life" (Matt. 7:13-14).

IV. Right and Wrong Roads (Prov. 4:14-19)

The human will plays a large part in determining the way that we take. We are not compelled by fate to take either the high road or the low. Our course in life is the result of choice. Hence this teacher's powerful urgings, "Avoid it, pass not by it, turn from it, and pass away" (v. 15), or "pass on" (RSV).

1. How to walk aright (vv. 14-15).—The four actions of verse 15 provide needed advice on how to keep on the right road. The seductive wide gate, described by Jesus (Matt. 7:13), must be shunned. Those who hang around this gate, with all its appeal, are likely to enter it, and so find themselves on that broad way that leads to destruction. Therefore, *avoid* it. Some people flirt with temptation, seeing how near they can go to it without being caught in its toils, Don't do that, says this teacher, "pass not by it," keep away as far as possible from its enticements. But suppose someone has started on that wrong road. Is there any hope for these? The exhortation, "turn away from it" (RSV), offers hope of escape from a mistake already made. The Christian concept of conversion, being "turned around," certainly supports this position. Finally, the possibility of avoiding a wrong decision is made sure for those who *pass on,* turning their backs on the entrance to the wrong road and directing their steps toward the right.

2. Vivid contrasts (vv. 16-19).—Most people cannot sleep when they have a guilty conscience. Verse 16 describes corrupt individuals who take such delight in doing evil that they cannot sleep without this satisfaction. Verse 17 may mean that wickedness and violence are their food and drink, or that they obtain their food and drink by the pursuit of wickedness and violence. Such moral bankruptcy is not the immediate consequence of taking the wrong road, but it may be the final outcome. On the other hand, "The path of the righteous is like the light of dawn, which shines brighter and brighter until full day" (v. 18, RSV).

V. Body Language (Prov. 4:23-27)

The road we choose will determine how we behave, and behavior, whether right or wrong, involves our bodies in all their parts. Paul exhorted his Roman readers to show their lack of conformity with the ways of the world by presenting their "bodies a living sacrifice, holy, acceptable unto God" (Rom. 12:1-2). Our Old Testament wise man had the same idea in verses 23-27. He specifically mentions four body parts that must be disciplined in the ways of wisdom.

1. Heart (v. 23).—Our hearts are important to our physical well-being. The Hebrew concept of the heart as the seat of the intelligence and will accentuates the importance of keeping our hearts right with God. We are to love Him with all our heart, not in external activity only, but deep in our innermost beings.

2. Mouth (v. 24).—The Bible has much to say about the mouth and the tongue as instruments of good or evil. A "froward mouth" is one that talks out of both sides and therefore deliberately deceives. The apostle James wrote of the same mouth producing both "blessing and cursing," and added the comment, "My brethren, these things ought not so to be" (Jas. 3:10).

3. Eyes (v. 25). Many are led astray by their eyes. Instead of training them to "look straight before thee," they are allowed to wander and become powerful instruments of evil.

4. Feet (vv. 26-27).—The psalmist prayed, "Cause me to know the way wherein I should walk" (Ps. 143:8). Feet can carry us into the wrong places and undesirable company. On them we follow either the broad or narrow way. No counsel given in these chapters is more important than, "Take heed to the path of your feet" (v. 26, RSV).

APPLYING THE LESSON

I teach children.—President Ford, in a White House ceremony in 1976, honored a black woman teacher from North Carolina. The President asked her, "What subjects do you teach?" The seventh-grade teacher responded, "I don't teach subjects. I teach children."

Great teachers do not teach subjects; they teach children. Such teachers are essential to the passing of wisdom from one generation to another.

What are the qualities of a great teacher? Bruce Larson did an experiment with teachers in which they described the qualities of their most effective teachers. They agreed that great teachers: listen a lot; trust their students; spend time with their students; are honest enough to share their own problems with the students; spend time with students outside the classroom; they help the students to discover their gifts and skills.[1]

Teachers with such qualities are probably the kind of teachers the writer of Proverbs refers to.

The desire to learn.—Wisdom is communicated when teachers with the qualities listed above come in contact with students who have a desire to learn. In that combination of quality teaching and responsive listening, wisdom is imparted.

One man described the development stages a learner goes through. He wrote about the memorable significance of his third-grade teacher and how he came to love her and admire her. During that early period he learned how to love his teacher. Then he remembered in a later period an irascible professor in his college life who created in him a great love for English literature. He lifted the student above the initial level of love for teacher and inserted the second tier of love for literature. Then, the third stage was added when he was trying to complete his doctoral dissertation. A famous teacher was his main consultant on his dissertation. He did not see the professor very often. Finally, he submitted his thesis which was returned to him with four or five pencil marks on the first few pages indicating that at least the professor had looked at it. However, the student was not satisfied. So he made an appointment with another professor and asked his advice on his dissertation. A couple of weeks later the professor invited him to his home one night. The student noticed his manuscript on the professor's desk with marks on practically every page. The professor said, "I have read your work carefully. You must rewrite it. Your rhetoric and your expressions are inadequate. Your conclusions are good, but if you want to get the benefit of an education, you must rewrite it."

It took three months to rewrite it. But the young student said, "I love that man who lifted me above the love of the person of my teacher and who lifted me above the love of the subject. He chastened me to a love of excellence."

Suffering the consequences.—After a vain search for a parking space downtown, a man stopped in a no-parking area. Hurriedly he scrawled a note and tucked it under the windshield wiper: "I've circled this block five times and couldn't find a place. I have to keep this appointment or I'll lose my job. I'm sorry. Forgive us our transgressions."

When he came back he had a ticket and attached to it this note: "I've circled this block for twenty years and if I don't do this, I'll lose my job. I'm sorry, too. Lead us not into temptation."

Certain actions will result in certain consequences, and no misuse of the Bible will change that. Because certain choices will lead us down certain roads, we need to be careful how we chose.

Conscience out of commission.—How would you describe your conscience? One little boy said that a conscience is what makes you tell your mother before your sister does! A converted Indian declared that a conscience was a little three-concerned thing that hurt him when it turned around. But," he added, "if I keep on doing wrong, it will turn so much that the corners become worn off and it doesn't work anymore." The writer of Proverbs speaks of those whose conscience was out of commission from repeated sins.

TEACHING THE CLASS

Main Idea: Teaching and learning God's wisdom is a lifelong process to be pursued at all costs.

Suggested Teaching Aim: Learners will identify ways to pursue the wisdom of God and recommit themselves to the pursuit.

Introduce the Bible Study

Ask: What teacher do you remember best from your school days? What Sunday School teacher do you remember? Invite learners to talk with those sitting around them to share their response to these questions. Encourage them to remember why that person made an impression on them and to share that with their group.

A Teaching Outline

1. Focus on teacher-student roles.
2. Discover how Proverbs describes the teacher-student relationship and what is to be learned by the student.
3. State how this learning can be personally acquired.
4. Commit selves to pursuit of this learning.

After several minutes, share the comments in "I teach children" *(Applying the Lesson).* Ask: What were the qualities of the teachers that you remember that made them good teachers? Elicit response.

Continue by stating that for learning to be the most productive, a student with a desire to learn is needed. Share the description of the stages that one man went through found in "The desire to learn" *(Applying the Lesson).*

State that the study for today focuses on the student-teacher relationship in learning the wisdom of God. Invite learners to turn to Proverbs 4 to discover how it is described.

Search for Biblical Truth

Call on a learner who has previously agreed to read Proverbs 4:1-13 aloud from a modern speech translation. Invite other learners to listen to hear the words of a teacher to his student.

When the reading is finished, state that the passage discusses the relationship between the student and his teacher and also describes what is taught and how valuable the lessons are. Divide the group into three sections. Direct one group to review verses 1-4 and prepare to describe the relationship between the teacher and the student. Direct the second group to review verses 10-13 for additional information about the relationship between the student and the teacher. Direct group three to review verses 5-9 to discover what is taught and how the teacher views the value of the learning. All groups should be prepared to discuss their findings with the class after about ten minutes.

When group presentations are made, be certain that they include ideas such as these. The teacher is anxious to pass on the experience that his father gave as he taught him (vv. 1-4). The teacher is concerned for the well-being of the student and not just for what he teaches (vv. 4,10-12). The teacher regards the student as his own child (vv. 1,10). The curriculum is the Word of God and His wisdom (v. 5). God's wisdom and understanding are so valuable that they are to be pursued at all cost (v. 7). The results of having God's wisdom are worth the price (vv. 6,8-9).

Give the Truth a Personal Focus

Ask rhetorically: On a scale of 1 to 10 how would you rate your desire to have the knowledge and the wisdom of God? Allow a brief time for learners to think about themselves. Continue by quoting verse 7 from the *New International Version:* "Wisdom is supreme; therefore get wisdom. Though it cost all you have, get understanding."

Ask: How can you get this wisdom of God? Are you to take the role of the student or the teacher? Is it possible that you are at times the student and at times the teacher? Are you a good teacher? Are you a good student? Why is it so important to continue to learn the wisdom of God?

Share "Conscience out of commission" found in *Applying the*

Lesson. Invite learners to commit themselves to pursuit of this learning.

1. Bruce Larson, *There's a Lot More to Health than Not Being Sick* (Waco: Word, 1981), p. 106.

July 8

Wisdom—The Creator's Delight

Basic Passage: Proverbs 8

Focal Passage: Proverbs 8:22-36

What is claimed to be the largest statue ever made stands in New York Harbor, the gift of France to the United States. It is the figure of a woman, torch in hand and with a broken chain beneath her feet. She is *Liberty.* Throughout our land, from Washington, D.C., to the farthest shores, another womanly figure is frequently seen, carved in stone. She is *Justice,* in one hand holding a balancing scale, in the other a sword. The practice of giving personality to abstract ideas is not strange to us but is freely accepted. The Bible presents Wisdom as a person, a woman, not in cold metal or stone but in well-chosen words that come to us with the stamp of inspiration. The highest tribute paid to her is found in our lesson passage in which Wisdom is described as the creation of God, associated with Him when He brought the universe into being. Eery new discovery made about earth, sea, or sky confirms the wisdom of the Creator and should strengthen our resolve to possess this wisdom for the discharge of less significant tasks that are our responsibility.

Study Aim: *To recognize evidence of divine wisdom in the physical universe and seek God-given wisdom for ourselves*

STUDYING THE BIBLE

Our lesson focuses on the second part of chapter 8, but the inclusion of the entire chapter in the basic material encourages us to enlarge the area of our study. The chapter falls into three parts: a renewed appeal to seek for wisdom; an exalted view of wisdom in its relationship to God; and a concluding exhortation.

I. Figures in Contrast (Prov. 8:1-9)

There is obvious contemporary value in the repeated warnings found in Proverbs against association with immoral persons. This emphasis is particularly strong in chapter 7 which vividly describes the seduction of a youth and its tragic consequences. In the absence of her husband (v. 19), a promiscuous woman invites a young man (v. 7) to share her bed. We are reminded of Joseph and Potiphar's wife (Gen. 39:7-20). Showing great moral strength, Joseph rejected the proposition made to him, and, as a consequence, was blessed by God so that he became second only to Pharaoh. But the victim in Proverbs succumbed to the temptation as "an ox goeth to the slaughter" (v. 22). Chapter 7 concludes with a warning against "the strange woman" (v. 5) whose "house is the way to hell, going down to the chambers of death" (v. 27).

1. Another woman's voice (8:1-3).—By contrast, Wisdom is introduced, not as operating "In the twilight, in the evening, in the black and dark night" (7:9), but openly extending her invitations in public places in the broad light of day. We have already met this picture of Wisdom's aggressive proclamation of her message (1:20-23).

2. Wisdom's wholesomeness (vv. 4-9).—There is nothing secretive about Wisdom's mission, neither is it addressed to naive and unwary individuals. In places of assembly, where crowds can be found, her message is sounded. Mature persons (v. 4) and the young and inexperienced ("simple," v. 5), even the hardnosed ("fools," v. 5), are exposed to the invitation. And the topics are "excellent things" and "right things" (v. 6). How clearly this anticipates the proclamation of the gospel to all sorts and conditions of people, to the receptive and unreceptive alike!

II. The Wealth of Wisdom (Prov. 8:11-18)

There are inducements in Wisdom's message, for the blessings promised are preferable to silver and gold and "better than rubies" (vv. 10-11). If we impose on these Old Testament statements a New Testament application, which we are surely entitled to do, then we may think of the treasures of the gospel as being beyond the value of precious metals and jewels.

1. "Witty inventions" (v. 12).—Taking these words at their face value, they remind us that the gift of divine wisdom enabled craftsmen, engaged in the construction of the tabernacle, to do their work with skill and excellence. It was persons "filled with the spirit of wisdom," who were employed to make Aaron's priestly garments (Ex. 28:2-4). Also Bezaleel was "filled with the spirit of God, in wisdom, and in understanding, and in knowledge" to equip him to do ornate work in metal, stone, and wood (31:2-5). The wisdom commended in Proverbs can contribute immeasurably to the performance of our daily occupations. However, "witty inventions" is probably more accurately translated "discretion" (RSV) and refers to the ability to exercise good judgment. Those who possess wisdom make the right choices in life, and do not live to regret their actions.

2. Royal performance (vv. 15-16).—The comments immediately above are appropriate to these verses. Those who hold the highest responsibilities in civic life are dependent on wisdom to do a good job. We recall how Solomon asked God for wisdom that he might rule Israel well.

III. An Attribute of God (Prov. 8:22-31)

A natural reaction of the Christian reader is to see in the following verses a foreshadowing of Christ. New Testament similarities, as found for example, in John 1:1-3; Colossians 1:15-17; and Hebrews 1:2-3, can confirm this impression. Conservative scholars warn us, however, as to the extent with which we press this parallel. Wisdom is presented as "her" and "she" (8:2; 9:1), whereas the Colossian passage uses "him" and "he." Also, while in early Christian centuries it was popular to interpret Proverbs 8:22-31 as referring to Christ, heretical teachers used the same verses to repudiate the eternal existence of our Lord.

22 The Lord possessed me in the beginning of his way, before his works of old.

23 I was set up from everlasting, from the beginning, or ever the earth was.

24 When there were no depths, I was brought forth; when there were no fountains abounding with water.

25 Before the mountains were settled, before the hills was I brought forth:

26 While as yet he had not made the earth, nor the fields, nor the highest part of the dust of the world.

27 When he prepared the heavens, I was there; when he set a compass upon the face of the depth:

28 When he established the clouds above: when he strengthened the fountains of the deep:

29 When he gave to the sea his decree, that the waters should not

pass his commandment: when he appointed the foundations of the earth:

30 Then I was by him, as one brought up with him: and I was daily his delight, rejoicing always before him;

31 Rejoicing in the habitable part of his earth; and my delights were with the sons of men.

1. God's creation (vv. 22-30).—Using poetic language, these verses affirm the antiquity of wisdom as an attribute of God, possessed by Him from the beginning. She was brought into being before the work of creation was started and was His companion throughout, "When he prepared the heavens, I was there" (v. 27). This claim does not go further than that of Psalm 104:24: "O Lord, how manifold are thy works! in wisdom hast thou made them all," or Psalm 135:1,5: "O give thanks unto the Lord. To him that by wisdom made the heavens." The marvels of our universe, the rhythm of the seasons, the interdependence of all created things, all bear eloquent testimony to the wisdom of the Creator.

2. Delight of God and mankind (vv. 30-31).—We must depend on scholarly judgment for the meaning of the phrase rendered "one brought up with him." The King James Version marginal reference and the Revised Standard Version, offer the alternative, "a master workman." Marvin Tate considers it best to stay with the concept of a child, and writes, "Wisdom plays beside Yahweh, and in the world, as his child. She is the playmate of God and man, whose status is unparalleled in the whole creation. Her message to men is grounded in a unique relationship with Yahweh. She represents the joyful presence of Yahweh in the world."[1] Whichever interpretation we accept, there is nothing said about Wisdom in this entire passage that parallels the claim made for the divine Son, "All things were made by him; and without him was not any thing made that was made" (John 1:3). Colossians 1:16-17 is even more explicit, "For by him were all things created, that are in heaven, and that are in earth, visible and invisible, whether they be thrones, or dominions, or principalities, or powers: all things were created by him, and for him: And he is before all things, and by him all things consist." In short, the New Testament salute to the divine Son, eternally with the Father and His agent in creation, far exceeds any Old Testament claim made for Wisdom.

IV. The Way to Blessing (Prov. 8:32-36)

The exaltation of Wisdom in our lesson chapters is nearing an end. Before we proceed to our final study in this book, we would do well to remind ourselves once more of the significance of the repeated statement, "The fear of the Lord is the beginning of wisdom: and the knowledge of the holy is understanding" (9:10). Back of all the down-to-earth advice offered in Proverbs is the conviction that a right relationship with God is the basic requirement of wisdom. For our concluding verses in chapter 8 we listen to the voice of Wisdom as God's personified attribute.

> **32 Now therefore hearken unto me, O ye children: for blessed are they that keep my ways.**
>
> **33 Hear instruction, and be wise, and refuse it not.**
>
> **34 Blessed is the man that heareth me, watching daily at my gates, waiting at the posts of my doors.**
>
> **35 For whoso findeth me findeth life, and shall obtain favour of the Lord.**
>
> **36 But he that sinneth against me wrongeth his own soul: all they that hate me love death.**

1. Nearing a conclusion (v. 32).—There are seven divisions in the Book of Proverbs, several easily recognizable by their introductions (10:1; 25:1). These different collections were brought together at a date hard to determine. The chapter divisions were not there originally, so that when the compiler of the first division (1:1 to 9:17) reached the verses printed above, he knew he was approaching the end of this remarkable statement on wisdom. He saw reason to renew his invitation to seek wisdom for all the blessings it bestows.

2. Eager seekers (vv. 33-36).—The previous chapter concludes with an implied warning to keep away from the house of an evil woman, for "her house is the way to hell, going down to the chambers of death" (7:27). A strikingly different situation prevails in the final verses of chapter 8 which pictures people clamoring to enter the doors of a place, perhaps a schoolhouse, where wisdom is taught. Clearly, the ways of wisdom are the ways of God, for the promise is given that those who seek and find wisdom will "obtain favour of the Lord." Where is wisdom to be found? Not in the Book of Proverbs alone, but in the Word of God in its entirety. Paul urged the reading of the Scriptures which, he wrote, "are able to make thee wise unto salvation through faith which is in Christ Jesus" (2 Tim. 3:15).

APPLYING THE LESSON

Following the crowd.—I remember a trick question on one of my tests during elementary school. The teacher would ask, "If twenty sheep were in a field, and one went to the other field, how many would be left?" The answer I put was nineteen which showed I knew about subtraction but not about sheep. The real answer was, "None," for if one sheep went to the adjoining field, all of the rest of the sheep would follow. Sheep and people have this tendency to follow the crowd. The writer of Proverbs focuses on this tragic habit of man.

Things haven't changed.—*Time* magazine reported: "One great educator became so infuriated with what he called the licentious, outrageous, disgraceful behavior of students at his college that he quit in disgust." The college was at Carthage. The year was 383 BC. The dismayed professor was Saint Augustine. Things have not changed all that much from the day of Augustine or from the time when Proverbs was written. In every generation, among all people, immorality is an ever-present temptation.

The source of wisdom.—Years ago a police officer in New York often stopped in to speak to Morty who was the proprietor of a delicatessen in the lower East Side of New York. "What makes Jewish people so smart?" the policeman asked. Morty looked both ways, leaned over to the police officer, and whispered, "I'll tell you a secret. It's because we eat so much pickled herring." The policeman was deeply impressed, so for the next six months he ate pickled herring every evening at Morty's delicatessen. Then one afternoon he stormed into the delicatessen, burning with anger. "Look here, Morty," he said, "for six months you have been charging me forty cents for a serving of pickled herring, and I just found out that I can get an even bigger portion around the corner for thirty cents." "What did I tell you?" grinned Morty. "The herring is working already!"

What does make people smart? Not pickled herring. Real wisdom comes form God. It is available to all who ask.

At the foot of the cross.—Dale Evans once summarized her Christian testimony in this one sentence: "All of my life I looked for a pot of gold at the end of the rainbow, but I found it at the foot of the cross."[2]

All of history's search for meaning ended in a dead-end street until Jesus came. All of the world's wisdom was foolishness until Jesus came. All of the world's power was weakness until Jesus came. His is indeed the name which is above every name.

The source of all wisdom.—Where is wisdom to be found? We find it in the revelation of God through His Word. A beautiful demonstration of this was given by Bill Burster. He met John during his sophomore year in college. He became good friends with this student from Nigeria. One day Bill asked him how he became a Christian. The young man answered, "When I was a little boy, running around in the bush country of Nigeria, I knew there was a God. I would stand among the trees and look up at the skies at night and know that someone made this world. I knew there was a God, but I didn't know what to call him. One day Josephine Skaggs, a Southern Baptist missionary, came to our village to teach us children how to read. She taught us how to read the Bible. There I discovered the name of the God who had revealed himself to me through the trees and stars."[3]

How do we discover the name of God, the purpose of God, the plan of

God for our lives, the rules by which we are to live? How do we discover the wisdom that will enable us to live productive Christian lives? We find that wisdom in the Bible.

The Bible is, as one man has called it, the manufacturer's handbook for better living. Fulfillment will come if you follow these simple admonitions in relationship to the Bible: dig it up, write it down, pray it in, live it out, and pass it on.

TEACHING THE CLASS

Main Idea: Wisdom is an attribute of God and should therefore be gained through Him.

Suggested Teaching Aim: Learners will acknowledge wisdom as an attitude of God which can also be theirs.

Introduce the Bible Study

Introduce the concept of representation through metaphors by using information from the introduction to *Studying the Bible*. If possible, display pictures of the *Statute of Liberty* and discuss what she represents. Note that the study for today represents the wisdom of God in poetic metaphor.

Recall that writings from the Proverbs studied in the last few lessons have focused on wisdom and its valuc. State that many seek for wisdom whether they know its source to be God or not. Share the story "The source of wisdom" found in *Applying the Lesson*.

Invite learners to turn in their Bibles to Proverbs 8 to study the beautiful poetry and to learn more about this quality of God called wisdom.

Search for Biblical Truth

Call on a learner who has previously agreed to do so to read Proverbs 8:22-36 aloud from a modern speech translation. Invite learners to listen to the poetic form in which this quality of God is presented.

Display the following outline to guide the study of the passage.

WISDOM—AN ATTRIBUTE OF GOD

I. The History of Wisdom—A Poetic Picture
   1. Before the world began (vv. 22-23).
   2. Before any of these (vv. 24-29).
   3. At His side (v. 30).
   4. Rejoicing and delighting (vv. 30-31).

II. The Admonition of Wisdom—A Way to Blessing
   1. Hear my instruction (vv. 32-33).

2. Blessings of wisdom (vv. 34-35).
3. Consequences of resistance (v. 36).

Call attention to the first item on the outline. Invite a learner to read aloud again verses 22-23. Emphasize that wisdom is an attribute of God that was in place before any of the creation of the world was begun.

Direct learners to review verses 24-29 to discover the things of creation listed there that wisdom preceeded. Encourage them to note and enjoy the poetic form of the writing. After several minutes, invite learners to list the things of creation which wisdom preceded. Ask: What point is the writer emphasizing with this statement? Elicit response. (The point is that wisdom always was a part of God and is therefore much to be desired and valued.)

A Teaching Outline

1. Focus on metaphoric representations.
2. Discover the history of wisdom and the admonitions of wisdom in the metaphoric representation of Proverbs.
3. Acknowledge personal need for and the value of having the wisdom of God as our own.

Call attention to items 3 and 4 of outline section I. Invite a learner to read verses 30-31 aloud while other learners listen for the work of wisdom in the creation of the earth. Call for response.

Direct attention to section II of the outline. Note that the personifed Wisdom admonishes to hear the instruction of God in verses 32-33. Allow time for learners to review the verses. Share the story "The source of all wisdom" found in *Applying the Lesson.*

State that the personified Wisdom goes on to state the blessings and consequcnces of accepting or refusing to learn the wisdom of God. Call on a learner to read verses 34-36 aloud.

Give the Truth a Personal Focus

Ask rhetorically: Have you considered that wisdom is a charactertistic of God that can be yours? have you accepted God's instructions or rejected them? The choice is yours.

---

1. Marvin E. Tate, *The Broadman Bible Commentary,* Volume 5 (Nashville: Broadman Press, 1971), p. 33.
2. Paul Powell, *The Complete Disciple* (Wheaton, IL: Victor Books, 1982), p. 101.
3. James E. Hightower, Compiler, *Illustrating Paul's Letter to the Romans* (Nashville: Broadman Press, 1984), p. 20.

Lessons from Life

Basic Passage: Proverbs 22:1-16

Focal Passage: Proverbs 22:1-16

A review of Bible passages selected for study over the past twenty years, reveals a scant use of the Book of Proverbs. This is understandable. So far our lessons have had a unifying theme, the subject of wisdom. But when we get into the heart of the book, we find a change in style. Its truths are not presented in an organized fashion, but as brief, self-standing statements that have been assembled without any attempt to group them into categories. As a result, each verse may feature a new subject, having little or no relation to what precedes or follows. This, of course, makes for variety, and variety for interest, but at the same time presents difficulties to any who seek to outline the material. In consequence of this, the following comments are not organized under headings, but under verses, majoring for the most part on those verses that speak to the situation and need of persons today.

Study Aim: *To submit our conduct to biblical teaching that we may exemplify the true meaning of "the fear of the Lord"*

STUDYING THE BIBLE

A new literary style is apparent in Proverbs 22, namely, the couplet (two lines of verse). This poetic form is introduced at 10:1 and continues through 22:16, this entire passage being described as "The Proverbs of Solomon" (10:1). Each couplet makes a single point. Sometimes the two lines express the same thought, but in different words. With others, contrasted, even conflicting, ideas are presented. There is a third form in which a second line continues the thought of the first. Part of our study could be to look out for these three variations and identify them. Examples, in the same order, may be found in 18:16; 14:11; and 18:13. Another matter of interest is that this collection of proverbs under the name of Solomon concludes at 22:16. Unfortunately, the chapter division does not recognize this. But a careful reading of 22:17-21 reveals that an introduction is being provided to a new collection of wise sayings. This section continues to 24:34. The beginning of another section is then clearly indicated by the words, "These are also proverbs of Solomon, which the men of Hezekiah king of Judah copied out" (25:1). To observe these things will help in understanding the process by which the Book of Proverbs was assembled, as we have it today. We now proceed with comments on the assigned verses (22:1-16).

1 A good name is rather to be chosen than great riches, and loving favour rather than silver and gold.

2 The rich and poor meet together: the Lord is the maker of them all.

The "good name" that is more desirable than "great riches" is indicative of social appreciation and acceptance. By implication, then, a poor person may enjoy the wealth of friendly relationships ("loving favour"). Character rather than possessions is the true means for obtaining recognition from others. Verse 2 has no clear link with verse 1, but it is appropriately placed. It affirms that rich and poor live together, they are major ingredients of society. Judged by appearances, they are widely different. But they have one thing in common: they are all the creatures of God. This thought is not developed, but one of the purposes of these pithy sayings is to stimulate our thinking. In light of the statement made about rich and poor, what conclusions do we reach?

3 A prudent man foreseeth the evil, and hideth himself: but the simple pass on, and are punished.

Another version is: "A prudent man sees danger and hides himself; but the simple go on, and suffer for it" (RSV). As motorists, we are encouraged to practice defensive driving, that is, to anticipate problems before they occur, and avoid them. That is a good principle for all of life. The word "prudent" means shrewd, or knowledgeable. The "simple" person, as we have already learned, is immature and naive. Interestingly enough, "are punished" can be literally rendered "are fined," which fits in with the idea of careless driving!

4 By humility and the fear of the Lord are riches, and honour, and life.

5 Thorns and snares are in the way of the froward: he that doth keep his soul shall be far from them.

These are contrasting verses. The association of "humility" and "the fear of the Lord," in verse 4, is a reminder that an inflated self-opinion can get in the way of a right relationship with God.

There are few human traits more frequently rebuked in the Bible than pride. King Saul was reproved by Samuel with these words, "When thou wast little in thine own sight, wast thou not made the head of the tribes of Israel, and the Lord anointed thee king over Israel? . . . Wherefore then didst thou not obey the voice of the Lord?" (1 Sam. 15:17,19). The "froward" of verse 5 are persons perverse and self-willed. The humble individual receives God-given honors, while the prideful reaps "thorns and snares."

6 Train up a child in the way he should go: and when he is old, he will not depart from it.

Experience teaches us that this is not an inflexible rule. Most church fellowships know the heartbreak of children raised in Christian homes who turn their backs on everything they have been taught. They fall prey to the influence of an increasingly secular society that often derides spiritual values. The optimism of verse 6 reflects the religious culture of the times, in which young and old were encouraged to keep God's law. Prevailing conditions today emphasize the importance of training the young in right ways by both instruction and discipline. Foundations of faith and morality that are early laid are likely to weather the storm.

7 The rich ruleth over the poor, and the borrower is servant to the lender.

These words were written at a time when there were no credit cards or second mortgages. But there were moneylenders, and it was not difficult to see that they were wealthy while their customers were poor. Today the so-much-a-month syndrome has millions in its toils; people whose piled-up debts make them the slaves of the system. Good stewardship for the Christian involves not only proportionate giving to the Lord, but the wise use of the balance.

8 He that soweth iniquity shall reap vanity: and the rod of his anger shall fail.

9 He that hath a bountiful eye shall be blessed; for he giveth of his bread to the poor.

We may be grateful for this rendering, "If you plant the seeds of injustice, disaster will spring up, and your oppression of others will end. Be generous and share your food with the poor. You will be blessed for it" (GNB). Dead tyrants and exiled dictators witness to the truth of verse 8. Recent times have provided plenty of examples. But one does not have to rule a banana republic to come under this condemnation. There are many situations in life in which people are exploited and oppressed. Those responsible need to be warned of the working of divine justice. How much better are the "bountiful" (v. 9), the compassionate and generous, who enjoy the approval of God!

10 Cast out the scorner, and contention shall go out; yea, strife and reproach shall cease.

11 He that loveth pureness of heart, for the grace of his lips the king shall be his friend.

12 The eyes of the Lord preserve knowledge, and he overthroweth the words of the transgressor.

All three verses have to do with words, their use and abuse. When a community, or group of any sort, is threatened with division because of a "scorner," or "scoffer," a person of spiteful disposition and unbridled tongue, the remedy is to exclude that individual. This speaks to the difficult subject of church discipline. Christian love would advise that extreme measures not be taken until every effort has been made to redeem the offender. The troublemaker is sharply contrasted to the person "whose speech is gracious" (v. 11, RSV). He does not make enemies but friends, even gaining the affection of a person as exalted as a king. The opening words of verse 12 have difficulties for the translator, but the rest of the verse is plain. God Himself takes note of those who offend with their words and will deal with them in justice. The opposite truth is to be found in "they that feared the Lord spake often one to another: and the Lord hearkened, and heard it" (Mal. 3:16).

13 The slothful man saith, There is a lion without, I shall be slain in the streets.

14 The mouth of strange women is a deep pit: he that is abhorred of the Lord shall fall therein.

More talk about talk. "Any excuse is better than none" is the meaning of verse 13. Here is a man, too lazy to get out of bed and go to work, who says that there is a lion in the street. The verse has an obviously humorous intent. Ridicule can sometimes get results when everything else fails. From the foolish talk of this verse we move on to the seductive talk of verse 14. In an earlier description of the ways of a prostitute with an unwary young man we read, "With her much fair speech she caused him to yield, with the flattering of her lips she forced him" (7:21). Perhaps we should remember that when Jesus dealt with a woman taken in adultery, it was to men that He said, "He that is without sin among you, let him first cast a stone at her" (John 8:7). The second part of Proverbs 22:14 should be understood to say that the man who yields is "abhorred of the Lord" because of, and not prior to, his sin.

15 Foolishness is bound in the heart of a child; but the rod of correction shall drive it far from him.

Somebody who knew boys was responsible for this verse. If they are healthy, they are full of mischief. Current disagreement over paddling a child must take account of this and other biblical injunctions to administer corporal punishment for purposes of discipline.

16 He that oppresseth the poor to increase his riches, and he that giveth to the rich, shall surely come to want.

This rendering is helpful: "He who oppresses the poor to increase his own wealth, or gives to the rich, will only come to want" (RSV). Both actions are exploitive. They seek personal gain by using other people. In the first case, the defenseless are put under pressure, perhaps to make them work harder, and their employer gains the benefit. In the second, money is used to influence powerful people to show favor to the donor. In the end, neither of the courses achieves its purpose but leads to retribution. Divine justice prevails.

APPLYING THE LESSON

This is character.—A banker named Wallace Byrd had an experience with evangelist Billy Sunday. Sunday came to Byrd's town to conduct a crusade. Each night huge crowds gathered to hear the powerful preaching of Sunday, but Byrd had no interest in religion and refused to attend. But by some quirk of fate, Billy Sunday arranged for an account to be set up in Byrd's bank. Every day the account grew, and so did Byrd's animosity toward the evangelist. On the Monday after his crusade ended, Sunday came into the bank to settle his affairs. Among the checks from the previous night's collection was one for five dollars. That gave Byrd a chance to express some of his resentment. "Mr. Sunday," he said, "we can't honor this check." "Why not?" Sunday asked. "Because she has less than $5 in her account. She is a widow and is very poor." Sunday frowned at the check and Byrd saw the opportunity for an extra harpoon. "Actually," he continued, "we are holding a mortgage on her home for $1,500. We'll have to foreclose soon." Byrd hoped that would hit this money-grabbing charlatan where it would hurt him most. Sunday nodded and tore up the check. A moment later he laid a piece of paper in front of Byrd and asked, "Will you honor this?" It was a check made out for $1,500 and designated for the widow's mortgage. Byrd was shaken. He said, "Why are you doing this?" Sunday simply replied that "true Christianity demanded it."

When Sunday left, Byrd was deeply moved and shamed. This event marked the turning point of his life and the event that led to his becoming a Christian. He said, "I never heard Billy Sunday preach from the pulpit. His only sermon to me was a signature on a personal check." That's character: what a man is when the crowd isn't watching. The writer of Proverbs says to have character, to have a good name, is better than having money in the bank.

Be prepared.—The little boy walked around the general store, looking carefully at each shelf. Finally, the proprietor spotted him, walked over to him, and asked, "Is there something I can help you with?" "Yes," the boy said, "do you have any blank report cards?" There was a young man who was planning ahead. The biblical word "prudent" could be applied to him.

The pride of accomplishment.—A husband told his wife he would give her $500 if she would quit smoking. She accepted the challenge and quit smoking. Later he told her he would give her $1,000 if she would quit bragging about it! How often we become proud of our achievements.

Not bad, just stupid.—Many decades ago, a preacher made an evaluation of parents that is still applicable today. He said, "Most parents are not bad, but many of them are stupid. Ask the psychiatrists, then, what ruins children, twists their plastic lives, imposes on them inner handicaps which the finest skill often cannot remove, and they will say it is not so much bad parents—they are not so frequent—as stupid parents. And the crux of the matter lies here: they did not need to be stupid; there was plenty of information available if they had counted it as seriously a part of their obligation to be intelligent as to be kind."[1]

Loose talk costs preacher.—A false statement traced to three preachers and an unidentified psychologist led to a $150,000 defamation judgment award to the author of *I'm OK, You're OK,* Thomas A. Harris. A preacher referred to Harris's book at a youth rally in Chico, California and said, "Most people don't kmow that the the author of that book committed suicide two years ago and yet people are still practicing some of his philosophies." He got his information from a tape by an evangelist. The evangelist got his information from a tape recording of another preacher. That preacher received his information from a talk made by an industrial psychologist. Tom Harris charged that these remarks had pictured him as a madman and held him up to public ridicule. It all happened because one man quoted another man who quoted another man who quoted another man, and none of them ever bothered to check his sources to see if the information was true. Such is the destructive power of the uncontrolled tongue.

TEACHING THE CLASS

Main Idea: Basic principles for shaping life are found in Proverbs.

Suggested Teaching Aim: Learners will explore teachings from the Proverbs and determine their implications for their lives.

Introduce the Bible Study

Ask: Would you rather have rules or principles to live your life by? Why? Elicit response, asking for reasons for the stated choices. If the discussion does not produce this thought, note that rules might make life simpler but they are also limiting. Note also that principles have a broader application but require personal responsibility for that application.

State that the study for today deals with several *principles* from the Book of Proverbs. Note that the objective of the study is to identify those principles from the Proverbs and to determine how to apply them in our own lives today. Invite learners to open their Bibles to Proverbs 22.

Search for Biblical Truth

Use information from the introduction to *Studying the Bible* and from the first paragraphs of the section to provide information about the literary style of this portion of Proverbs. Note the change in style and the authorship.

A Teaching Outline

1. Introduce the style of the statements in this part of Proverbs.
2. Explore the meaning of the individual proverbs.
3. Discover how these teachings can be applied to their lives.
4. Decide to live more productively, using the principles found in the Proverbs.

Write the word *couplet* on the chalkboard. Note the three styles of couplets mentioned while making the following notes on the chalkboard:

Form 1—Same thought, different words;
Form 2—Contrasted or conflicting ideas;
Form 3—Continuation of the thought in second line.

State that the couplets identified for study today will fall into one of these three styles.

Call on a learner to read the focal passage, Proverbs 22:1-16, while other learners listen, remembering the new poetic style being employed. When the reading is finished, remind learners of the purpose for this study.

Assign couplets as they are separated in *Studying the Bible*. There are ten divisions. Assign more than one to a person or group of persons, if necessary. Direct learners to read the couplet, identify the principle for living life, and identify ways the principle can be implemented in learners' lives today. Suggest that learners consult modern speech translations and/or write the verses in their own language. This should help to make the principle clear and applicable for today's living. After a period for study, call on learners to share their conclusions. Share the stories and remarks from *Applying the Lesson* in connection with the reports on the indicated verses. Verses 1-2—Share story titled "This is character." Verse 3—Share story titled "Be prepared." Verses 4-5—Share story titled "The pride of accomplishment." Verse 6—Share story titled "Not bad, just stupid." Verses 10-12—Share story titled "Loose talk costs preacher."

Give the Truth a Personal Focus

The following applications to learners' personal lives are suggestions and may be provided in addition to the applications learners will identify.

Verses 1-2: Work at establishing a good name through living by the golden rule. Know that this is what God honors.

Verse 3: Avoid evil influence that interferes with spiritual growth.

Verse 6: Do what you can to train a child in the right way. When he is old, it is a matter between him and God.

Verse 7: Before you borrow, decide to what extent the loan requires you to serve the lender and choose wisely.

Verses 10-12: Understand the power of words and learn to use them wisely.

Invite learners to live more productively by using these teachings in their lives.

---

1. H. E. Fosdick, *The Hope of the World* (New York: Harper and Brothers, 1933), p. 226.

July 22

Proverbs in Pictures

Basic Passage: Proverbs 30

Focal Passage: Proverbs 30:18-33

In the depository of wisdom that we know as the Book of Proverbs, we meet a man who had the courage to say, "I don't know." His name was Agur (30:1), and we know nothing about him except that he had sufficient reputation for his words to be included along with Solomon's. These are some of the things he said about himself, "Surely I am too stupid to be a man. I have not the understanding of a man. I have not learned wisdom, nor have I knowledge of the Holy One" (vv. 3-4, RSV). As we read on we realize that he was criticizing himself too severely. He was probably reacting to people who claimed superior knowledge. In his determination not to be overtaken by pride he overindulged in humility. But he qualified his professed ignorance when he affirmed, "Every word of God proves true" (v. 5, RSV). He had a remedy for his lack of knowledge, the Word of God. That remedy is available to us all.

Study Aim: *To develop inquiring minds that are open to instruction*

STUDYING THE BIBLE

Agur did not use couplets to express his thoughts, but paragraphs. He also resorted to the use of the numbers three and four, probably to make his teaching easier to remember. The prophet Amos used a similar verbal device in his repeated indictments, "For three transgressions . . . and for four" (Amos 1:3,6,9). Both men may have been saying, "I give you three or four examples. I could give you more."

I. Some Amazing Things (Prov. 30:18-20)

Reading these verses is like listening in on another person's thoughts. Agur has already acknowledged his lack of understanding. Now he expressed his thoughts on a number of things that perplex, amaze, or bother him. He begins with some observations about the world around him that may appear to have no spiritual or moral value, except, perhaps, verse 20. But they are evidence of an inquiring mind and a capacity for wonder. The latter is something we are all in danger of losing, so that life no longer has any surprises for us. To recover childhood's curiosity could lead to great discoveries—about ourselves, even about God.

> **18 There be three things which are too wonderful for me, yea, four which I know not:**
>
> **19 The way of an eagle in the air; the way of a serpent upon a rock; the way of a ship in the midst of the sea; and the way of a man with a maid.**
>
> **20 Such is the way of an adulterous woman; she eateth, and wipeth her mouth, and saith, I have done no wickedness.**

1. Causes for wonder (vv. 18-19).—The flight of an eagle is beautiful to watch. It floats on the air, rising and falling with the current, until it sees its prey, and then darts at lightning speed for the catch. Agur witnessed this with amazement, as was also the case with a very different creature, the serpent. What explanation was there for the way in which, without the aid of legs, the serpent moved freely and swiftly on the hard surface of a rock? Then this landlubber looked out to sea and marveled at the course of a ship which, with only sails to catch the wind, traveled from port to port. Finally, he found reason to confess his ignorance of the activity of love: how love arises between two persons, and how it expresses itself.

2. Carefree sinning (v. 20).—In the area of morals, Agur was surprised at the way some people transgress God's law with no twinges of conscience. He specifically mentioned an adulteress to whom indulging her passion was of no more consequence than eating a meal. This casual attitude toward sexual promiscuity is currently widespread. Live-in arrangements between members of the opposite sex do not raise an eyebrow. Agur did not take easily to such practices. Neither should we.

II. Some Troublesome Things (Prov. 30:21-23)

We have already realized that Agur did not mince words. He told things as he saw them. There are three things, no four, he said, that invariably cause trouble. Can we doubt that he listed them in the hope that others would be warned of these inflammatory situations, and, where possible, avoid them?

> **21 For three things the earth is disquieted, and for four which it cannot bear:**

22 For a servant when he reigneth; and a fool when he is filled with meat;

23 For an odious woman when she is married; and an handmaid that is heir to her mistress.

Promotion in life is so much a part of our American system as to raise questions in our minds about some of these observations. We need to understand them, not as a criticism of this system, but as a warning against giving advancement to persons whose dispositions are wrong. There are some persons who cannot be entrusted with authority, and when, by mistake, they are, they abuse the trust placed in them.

1. Unbearable men (vv. 21-22).—The earth "trembles" when "a slave . . . becomes king" (RSV). Persons of low degree have been given leadership responsibilities without losing their heads. The implied criticism here is of a person of slave mentality who somehow rises to kingship. Let others beware for he is likely to be a tyrant. The word translated "fool" only appears one other time (17:7). It does not refer to lack of intelligence but to someone despicable for his contempt of all that is desirable and good. When "he is filled with food" (RSV), or, as we might say, "strikes it rich," he can become a source of public danger.

2. Obnoxious women (v. 23).—There are problems of translation in this verse. For "odious" the Revised Standard Version has "unloved," and other offerings are "hateful" and "plain girl." Together these indicate the difficulties involved. Perhaps we should think of an underprivileged person, for whatever reason, who makes a good marriage. She does not know how to handle her newly acquired status, and others suffer the consequences. Of course, the opposite has been true. The fourth example, "a maid" who "succeeds her mistress" (RSV), is more easily understood. As her widowed boss's new wife she may get a swelled head. As a New Testament parallel, we might think of the apostle Paul's advice, "Lay hands suddenly on no man" (1 Tim. 5:22), by which he warned Timothy against giving church leadership responsibilities to a person who had not fully proved himself.

III. Some Wise Though Small Things (Prov. 30:24-28)

Agur was clearly a nature watcher. His object was not so much entertainment as instruction. He discovered that there is much to be learned from small creatures. As a "wise man" of his generation, whose thoughts were considered worthy to be included in a royal collection (1:1), he was probably the associate of kings and princes. He was clearly familiar with what went on in palaces

(30:28). But he did not confine importance to the big and influential. In God's world, little things can play significant roles.

24 There be four things which are little upon the earth, but they are exceeding wise:
25 The ants are a people not strong, yet they prepare their meat in the summer:
26 The conies are but a feeble folk, yet make they their houses in the rocks;
27 The locusts have no king, yet go they forth all of them by bands;
28 The spider taketh hold with her hands, and is in kings' palaces.

1. Industrious ants (v. 25).—Ants are mentioned only twice in the Bible, both times in Proverbs (6:6; 30:25). Reference is to a species of ants, known as harvesters, that nest near grainfields and depositories. They gather kernels at sowing time and also when the grain is harvested. On sunny days they are known to bring their store out from its underground barns so that it may dry in the warmth. Agur commended them for their foresight in making preparation for the winter.

2. Well-housed conies (v. 26).—The creature thus named is like a rabbit without the long ears. It is a species of hyrax, incorrectly named "badgers" (RSV). Though small and defenseless, it finds security by living in rocks.

3. Destructive locusts (v. 27).—There is no problem identifying locusts which were, and continue to be, a scourge in certain parts of the world. The eighth plague against Egypt consisted of locusts (Ex. 10:3-20). In several places in the Bible these insects symbolize powerful armies (Joel 2:4,6-7). They descend in millions on unharvested fields and strip them clean. They do this without leadership, instinctively cooperating in their prolonged flights and destructive activities. What they could not do alone, they accomplish together.

4. Intrusive lizards (v. 28).—The reference here is to lizards, not spiders (see RSV). They are small enough to hold in the hand (if you can catch them), but bold enough to enter kings' palaces. These small creatures are further illustration of the achievements possible to the insignificant and unimportant.

IV. Some Impressive Things (Prov. 30:29-33)

These are not all easy to describe, translators acknowledging that the Hebrew gives them trouble. Help may be had from various translators available.

29 There be three things which go well, yea, four are comely in going:

30 A lion which is strongest among beasts, and turneth not away for any;

31 A greyhound; an he goat also; and a king, against whom there is no rising up.

32 If thou hast done foolishly in lifting up thyself, or if thou hast thought evil, lay thine hand upon thy mouth.

3 Surely the churning of milk bringeth forth butter, and the wringing of the nose bringeth forth blood: so the forcing of wrath bringeth forth strife.

In his appreciation for the accomplishments of the small and the weak, Agur did not ignore the powerful and the strong. In verse 31 we may prefer, "the strutting cock, the he-goat, and a king striding before his people" (RSV), though for "people" we could read "armies." Any of these can be impressive in bearing and performance. So Agur found reason for admiring little and great, obscure and prominent. All things can find their place in the divine plan and purpose. But this is not reason for pride on the part of any, hence verse 32. "If you have been foolish, exalting yourself, or if you have been devising evil, put your hand on your mouth" (RSV). This is what Job did after granted an experience of the greatness of God. "I will lay mine hand upon my mouth," he said (Job. 40:4). There is a time for quietness and contemplation; and the Book of Proverbs gives us reason for both.

APPLYING THE LESSON

The spirit of adventure.—The little boy was dressed for Sunday School in his new white outfit. Now his mother could finish getting dressed. When she finished getting ready, she looked outside to see her little boy, in his white suit, sitting up in a tree. She ran outside and commanded the child to come down. Grabbing the child by the shoulders, the mother shouted, "Why in the world would you climb up into a tree after I had dressed you for Sunday School?" The little boy said, "I just climbed up to see what I could see." That spirit of adventure, missing from most of us today, is revealed in the man named Agur.

The real moral dilemma today.—Elton Trueblood quotes Will Herberg from Drew University on the moral crisis of our day. Herberg said that the trouble today is not that Americans break the moral laws with great frequency. The real problem is the rejection of the conception that there is any moral law to break.[1]

This is not a new development. Three thousand years ago, people lived as if there were no moral laws to break.

A true leader.—Concerning what it takes to be a leader: In 2 Timothy

Paul gave a summary statement: "For God hath not given us the spirit of fear; but of power, and of love, and of a sound mind" (1:7). "Power" is the strength by which we are led. "Love" is the spirit in which we are to lead. "Sound mind" is the good sense with which we are to lead. When a person is exalted to a leadership position without the tools of leadership—strength, spirit, and sense—the result will be trouble.

The power of the small.—Dr. Harry Grattan Guinness told about the time when the water supply became choked out of their college in Derbyshire, England. They could not obtain a drop of water in the entire building. They searched the cisterns and inspected the taps and the whole machinery, but could find no cause for the problem. Finally, they went to the junction that connected the pipe from the reservoir with the pipe going into the house. They discovered a toad blocking the pipe. They were told that he had probably come into the water system as a tadpole, had fed upon the water, changed into a toad, grown in size, so that now the entire water supply was stopped because of him. Small things can do great damage.

The power of persistence.—More than 15,000 runners entered the New York City Marathon in October, 1982. The race started at 10:30 AM. Seven hours later, 13,609 runners had completed the twenty-six-mile course. Darkness began to fall and cleanup crews were taking down the barricades and sweeping up the litter. But the race wasn't over yet. A lone woman, her aluminum crutches glinting in the streetlights, was still making her way along the course. Linda Downs, born with cerebral palsy, was determined to finish the race. Six times she fell during the race, but each time she got up and kept going. Someone alerted the television station and a camera crew began to follow her slow progress. Strangers, as well as family, lined the street and cheered her to the finish line. Finally, after more than eleven hours, Linda crossed the finish line. Like the creatures in Agur's list who were small but significant, Linda overcame her physical disability through persistence to make her mark.

The source of all true greatness.—One of the greatest hymns of Christendom is the one written by John Newton, profligate slave captain who was transformed by the redeeming power of Jesus Christ. The hymn tells the story of his marvelous turnaround. However, it does not tell the story of the accomplishments John Newton made for Christ after his conversion. He became a great preacher and an effective communicator of the gospel. However, he never thought of his achievements as something he did. He also recognized that the source of his power and productiveness was Jesus Christ. To help him remember the true source of his accomplishments, John Newton had written over the door in his study so that he would view it again every day: "Thou shalt remember that thou wast a bondman in the land of Egypt and the Lord God redeemed thee."

TEACHING THE CLASS

Main Idea: There is much to be learned from observing and thinking about the things around you.

Suggested Teaching Aim: Learners will explain the observations and thoughts of the writer of these Proverbs and determine the advantages of an inquiring mind in their relationship with God.

Introduce the Bible Study

Tell the incident found in "The spirit of adventure" in *Applying the Lesson.* Ask: Why are children more inclined to act on their curiosity than adults? Are children more curious than adults? What would be the advantage for an adult of developing a curious mind? Would it be appropriate for an adult to take action to satisfy his curiosity? Elicit response, inviting learners to think and share differing points of view.

Continue: In what ways could a curious mind affect a person's relationship with God? Why would it be an advantage or a disadvantage? Elicit brief response.

Use information from the introduction to *Studying the Bible* and from the first paragraphs of the same section to introduce the person Agur. Share information about the change in style and the probable authorship of this section of Proverbs.

A Teaching Outline

1. Consider the effect of childlike curiosity.
2. Discover and explain the wonderings and conclusions of Agur as he observed those things around him.
3. State the advantages of an inquiring mind for an improved relationship with God.

State the title of the lesson for today. Note that the purpose of the pictures is to give us insight into God's plans and principles for His creation. State that the purpose for the study today is to help us understand these pictures and to develop similar curious observation of God's world around us.

Search for Biblical Truth

Invite learners to read Proverbs 30:18-20 to themselves and be ready to describe the pictures the verses create in their minds. When finished, call for responses. Write "Some Amazing Things" on the chalkboard.

Continue by asking questions like the following: What four things were a curiosity for Agur? Have you ever been puzzled or awed by them? What is the picture created by verse 20? Share the story "The real moral dilemma today" *(Applying the Lesson).*

Write "Some Troublesome Things" on the chalkboard. Invite learners to read Proverbs 30:21-23 to themselves and be ready to share the pictures that the words of Agur create in their minds. When finished, call for response.

Ask questions like the following. Why would the coming of a servant to a place of power be a troublesome thing? What might the meaning of "fool" be other than one who lacks intelligence? (Share information from *Studying the Bible*.) What is the meaning of the word "odious"? Why is an odious woman a troublesome thing? What problems might be created by a handmaid becoming heir to her mistress?

Write "Some Things Wise and Small" on the chalkboard. Direct learners to read verses 24-28 to themselves to discover why Agur observed these small things to be wise. When finished, call for response. Share the stories "The power of the small" and "The power of the persistent" (*Applying the Lesson*).

Write "Some Things Great and Strong" on the chalkboard. Direct learners to read Proverbs 30:29-33 to discover the four things which Agur observed to be great and strong. Call for response.

Continue by asking: What is the advice of Agur in verses 32-33? Share the information in "The source of all true greatness" found in *Applying the Lesson*.

Give the Truth a Personal Focus

Ask: What effect could having a curious mind that observes what goes on around you have on your relationship with God?

---

1. Elton Trueblood, *A Place to Stand* (New York: Harper, 1969), p. 16.

July 29

All Is Vanity

Basic Passage: Ecclesiastes 1:1 to 2:26

Focal Passages: Ecclesiastes 1:2-8,12-17; 2:24-25

Ecclesiastes is strictly an Old Testament book. Its outlook, except for an occasional reference to God (always significant), is limited to things "under the sun" (1:14). The appearance of contradictory statements is probably due to the fact that the writer assumes the role of a person who is materialistically minded, but occasionally allows his better feelings, as a man of faith, to break through. But even at his best, this writer is confined in his thinking by the prevailing ignorance of an afterlife, which caused Clyde T. Francisco to say, "If there is no afterlife, then the present life is in the main a drab, colorless, aimless existence. As one reads the book, he is made eternally grateful for the assurance of immortality provided by Jesus Christ." In spite of its inadequacies, Francisco pointed out, Ecclesiastes maintains that "in this life it pays to serve God. God's rewards come in the present as well as the future. To the one who serves him, he gives an added capacity to live life to its fullest."[1]

Study Aim: *To put a true value on the things of this world and learn to accept even simple pleasure as gifts from God*

STUDYING THE BIBLE

Who was "the preacher" whose words are preserved in this book? (1:1). He is described as "the son of David, king in Jerusalem," which suggests Solomon. This opinion may seem to be confirmed by the statement, "I the Preacher was king over Israel in Jerusalem" (v. 12). But the past tense of this statement raises a problem. Solomon reigned until his death (1 Kings 11:41-43). Therefore, there was never a time when he could say that he "was king." The solution, accepted by conservative scholars, is that in Ecclesiastes an anonymous writer put his words into the deceased Solomon's mouth. There are indications in the book that it was a product of a much later age than Solomon's.

I. Is All of Life Futile? (Eccl. 1:2-8)

The biblical account of Solomon shows a man who lived life to the full, after the style of an Eastern monarch. "Now the weight of gold that came to Solomon in one year was six hundred threescore and six talents of gold. . . . Moreover the king made a great throne of ivory, and overlaid it with the best gold. . . . So king Solomon exceeded all the kings of the earth for riches and for wisdom" (1 Kings 10:14,18,23). For this indulgent life-style see 11:1-3. He was a fitting subject of which to ask, "Can possessions and pleasures bring real satisfaction?" The answer was a resounding no.

2 Vanity of vanities, saith the Preacher, vanity of vanities; all is vanity.
3 What profit hath a man of all his labour which he taketh under the sun?
4 One generation passeth away, and another generation cometh: but the earth abideth for ever.
5 The sun also ariseth, and the sun goeth down, and hasteth to his place where he arose.
6 The wind goeth toward the south, and turneth about unto the north; it whirleth about continually, and the wind returneth again according to his circuits.
7 All the rivers run into the sea; yet the sea is not full; unto the place from which the rivers come, thither they return again.
8 All things are full of labour; man cannot utter it: the eye is not satisfied with seeing, nor the ear filled with hearing.

1. Contrasted conditions.—The people to whom Solomon, as "The Preacher," was pictured as addressing his thoughts lived under very different conditions from those he enjoyed. There are repeated references in Ecclesiastes to oppression and suffering. The point made was that if they lived in a state of futility approaching despair, so also did he. As the royal "wise man" of his people he concluded that if this life is all, it has little to offer in enduring satisfaction. He had other thoughts, as we shall see; but the basic message of this book is the emptiness of life at the secular level. "Vanity of vanities . . . all is vanity" (v. 1). The repeated word creates a superlative—utmost, or absolute vanity.

2. What goes around, comes around (vv. 2-8).—What is the ultimate end of human effort, no matter of what sort? From a king governing his kingdom, to a person engaged in forced labor, the result is frustration. We live and die, and another generation takes our place. Nature itself operates in circles: the sun in its course from sunrise to sunset, repeated without end; the wind in its variableness, blowing first one way and then another; rivers that run their course only to lose their identity in the sea. To many people, this is all there is to existence. But not to the Christian. The dejection reflected in these pessimistic thoughts needs the corrective remedy of the gospel of Jesus Christ.

II. Search for an Answer (Eccl. 1:12-17)

The title "Ecclesiastes" comes from the Latin and Greek versions of this book. We are familiar with the term *ecclesia,* sometimes translated "church," and meaning an assembly of people. In Greek, an *ecclesiastes* was a teacher of such a group, hence, "the Preacher." The Hebrew word behind this is *Koheleth,* which comes from a root meaning "to call," or "to assemble."

12 I the Preacher was king over Israel in Jerusalem.

13 And I gave my heart to seek and to search out by wisdom concerning all things that are done under heaven: this sore travail hath God given to the sons of man to be exercised therewith.

14 I have seen all the works that are done under the sun; and, behold, all is vanity and vexation of spirit.

15 That which is crooked cannot be made straight: and that which is wanting cannot be numbered.

16 I communed with mine own heart, saying, Lo, I am come to great estate, and have gotten more wisdom than all they that have been before me in Jerusalem: yea, my heart had great experience of wisdom and knowledge.

17 And I gave my heart to know wisdom, and to know madness and folly: I perceived that this also is vexation of spirit.

1. Disappointing quest (vv. 12-15).—With the advantage of his position, and his reputed wisdom, Solomon is made to say that he had made a careful study of all human activity. His conclusion was that everything was "an unhappy business" (v. 13, RSV). Human achievement is not denied; but, of whatever kind it is, the ultimate judgment is that it is "a striving after wind" (v. 14, RSV). Efforts to change conditions are themselves in vain. "That which is crooked cannot be made straight: and that which is wanting cannot be numbered" (v. 15). The flaw in all this reasoning is that it leaves God out. The value for the reader is that it portrays the aimlessness of life that is not God-directed.

2. Different aspects (vv. 16-17).—Again claiming exceptional advantages, the Preacher told how he looked at two life-styles, that which followed wisdom and that which took the path of folly. Certainly in his lifetime, Solomon adopted both these courses. He declared that both were "striving after wind" (v. 17, RSV). There is no judgment here concerning the rightness and wrongness of human behavior, only a conclusion that either course brings disappointment. His meaning on one issue is clarified by verse 18, "For in much wisdom is much grief: and he that increaseth knowledge increaseth sorrow." This is not an "ignorance is bliss" position, but a frank acknowledgment that the more we know about life in general the more aware we become of its tragedies and disillusionments. Though this is far from a Christian attitude, most of us will find a measure of empathy with the writer's conclusions.

III. Can Pleasure Satisfy? (Eccl. 2:1-11)

With all of chapters 1 and 2 as background material, we do well to give attention to these verses. In his quest for enduring satisfaction, the Preacher decided to explore all aspects of the good life. Before detailing his activities, he stated his ultimate conclusion: "This also is vanity" (v. 1). As readers, we are warned in advance that, no matter how glamorous or appealing selfish enjoyment may be, it cannot satisfy the deeper yearnings of the heart.

1. Indulgent living (v. 3).—"I searched with my mind how to cheer my body with wine—my mind still guiding me with wisdom—and how to lay hold on folly" (RSV). He did not engage in drunkenness, but sought to discover the pleasures of wine, all the time exercising the restraint that wisdom imposes. In modern terms we would probably say he became a gourmet, an expert in good food. All the pleasures that go with fancy dining were also explored, but to no good purpose.

2. Extravagant projects (vv. 4-8).—Possessed by the means to do these things, he tried to find fulfillment in great buildings, beautiful gardens, planned irrigation, well-stocked farms, musical instruments, and male and female singers, with still enough money over to have hoards of silver and gold. The extravagant excesses of wealthy people today, whose indulgent life-styles are frequently exhibited in television programs, could move us to envy. But the experience of the Preacher was that all this luxury brought no contentment.

3. Passing pleasure (vv. 9-11).—There was momentary satisfaction while all these projects were being worked out: "My heart found pleasure in all my toil, and thus was my reward for all my toil" (v. 10, RSV). This acknowledgment gives a basis of reality to these recollections. People work on pretentious plans and get satisfaction while the work is in process. But they are seldom satisfied. One achievement must be followed by another, and another.

To stop and think would compel admission that "all was vanity and a striving after wind" (v. 11, RSV).

IV. Give God the Praise (vv. 24-25)

We are not to assume that the activities described in the early verses of chapter 2 are essentially evil. The reason they brought no enduring satisfaction was that God had no place in these enterprises. He was neither consulted nor thanked. But in the verses below a change in attitude is revealed.

> **24 There is nothing better for a man, than that he should eat and drink, and that he should make his soul enjoy good in his labour. This also I saw, that it was from the hand of God.**
> **25 For who can eat, or who else can hasten hereunto, more than I?**

Verse 25 becomes meaningful in this version, "For apart from him who can eat or who can have enjoyment?" (RSV). The emptiness of life as he has tried it brings the writer to the conclusion that to be content with simple pleasures—food and drink, and a job to do—and to acknowledge these as gifts from God, is the course to follow. Thus he takes a feeble step in the right direction, but still has a long way to go before the Christian motivation is within his grasp. The master said: "But seek ye first the kingdom of God, and his righteousness; and all these things shall be added unto you" (Matt. 6:33).

APPLYING THE LESSON

In sharp contrast.—The life of vanity described in the Book of Ecclesiastes of a man who has wealth but did not enjoy life stands in stark contrast to that of George Washington Carver. Carver had little that the world considers to be important, yet he experienced true life. About his life of discovery he testified, "I am God's servant, His agent, for here God and I are alone. I am just the instrument through which He speaks, and I would be able to do more if I were to stay in closer touch with Him. With my prayers I mix my labors, and sometimes God is pleased to bless the results." Is it any wonder that this epitaph marks the grave of this dedicated man of God: "He could have added fortune to fame, but caring for neither, he found happiness and honor in being helpful to the world."

The meaning of life.—A young man who had just become king desired to possess a survey of the universal history of mankind that he might learn its lessons. At the end of twenty years his learned men brought him a dozen camels, each bearing 500 volumes. The busy king said, "I do not have time to read all of that. Kindly abridge." After a long period of time, they came back to the king with a smaller edition of their work. Again he commanded,

"Please abridge it some more." Finally, his chief wise man brought to the king a single volume, only to find the king on his deathbed. As the now aged, failing king eyed the massive volume, he sighed in despair, "Alas, I shall die without ever knowing the history of mankind." "Your Majesty," said the scholar, "I will summarize it for you in three simple phrases: 'Men are born, they suffer, and they die.'"

Depression.—The spirit of Ecclesiastes prevails in our world today. One doctor suggests that depression is "the common cold of psychiatric ills." F. Scott Fitzgerald, the famous author, wrote during his periods of severe depression, "In a real dark night of the soul it is always three o'clock in the morning." Winston Churchill, the inimitable British leader, was often beset by what he called his "black dog" of depression. Dr. Frederic Flach, a medical doctor who specializes in depression, estimates that "approximately eight million Americas are in immediate need of professional help for their depression."

Dead-end street.—The road of pleasure does not lead to fulfillment but to further frustration. Joy returns only as we return to the Lord. This truth is beautifully illustrated in a story I heard many years ago. A certain man returned to his old homeplace after his mother died to sell the furnishings. Rummaging through the treasures in the attic, he came upon a brown box. His fingers restlessly tore at the wrappings. Inside he found two little shoes, turned yellow by the years. Attached to the shoes was a note: "Yesterday Thomas was two. I saw him standing in the sun with his new shoes. 'Oh, Mama,' he said, 'I'm standing in the smile of God.'"

Suddenly the summer sunlight flooded through the ancient oak trees. Memories returned suddenly like waves beating against the beach. He remembered graduating from high school. He remembered being at the top of his university class. He remembered being elected president of his firm. He thought again of his financial accomplishments. Then, he realized how through all of those experiences he had neglected God. The old note pricked his conscience, and suddenly he got down on his knees and prayed, "Blessed Lord, help me to stand once more in the smile of God."

Luck or trust?—In the mountains of North Carolina, less than five miles apart, are two tiny hamlets. One is named Trust and the other is named Luck. In a sense everyone lives in one of these two towns. We either live by luck or we live by trust. Those who live by luck never understand that behind every gift of life is the Giver. They never see themselves as a part of an overarching plan which God is working out. Those who live by trust recognize that every good and perfect gift comes from God.

TEACHING THE CLASS

Main Idea: This life has only emptiness apart from recognition of life as a gift from God.

Suggested Teaching Aim: Learners will assess their attitudes about the value of life in this world.

Introduce the Bible Study

Ask: What accomplishments or achievements in this life usually make persons feel that life is worthwhile? List responses on the chalkboard. They will probably include such things as graduating from school, having a family, having meaningful work, having friends, buying a home, traveling. Continue by posing these circumstances: If God is not a part of all of these things, how lasting are they? (They only last for the moments of the experience.) Continue by asking rhetorically: How can life have its fullest meaning? Allow a few moments for thought.

A Teaching Outline

1. Introduce the Book of Ecclesiastes and today's lesson.
2. Discover the Preacher's dilemma about the meaning of life.
3. Assess personal attitudes about the value of life in this world and accept it all as a gift from God.

State: The study for today will help us to look at life from another point of view. The purpose is to help us assess our own attitudes about this life and determine its value to us. Invite learners to turn in their Bibles to the Book of Ecclesiastes.

Search for Biblical Truth

Use information from *Studying the Bible* to introduce the Book of Ecclesiastes. An alternative is to enlist a class member to prepare a brief presentation about the book. Consider the author, the time of writing, the style of writing and the basic overall message of the book.

Display this outline to guide the Bible searching.

WHAT IS THE MEANING OF LIFE?

1. The question: Is all of life futile? (Eccl. 1:2-8).
2. A search for the answer (Eccl. 1:12-17).
3. Is pleasure the answer? (Eccl. 2:1-11).
4. A different perspective (Eccl. 2:24-25).

Share the story "The meaning of life" from *Applying the Lesson*. Call on a learner to read Ecclesiastes 1:2-8 aloud. Invite other learners to listen to learn the conclusion to which the Preacher comes when he asks whether all of life is futile. Call for response. Share the comments from "Depression" (*Applying the Lesson*). Ask: Why is the Preacher so depressed as he considers life?

Call attention to item 2 on the study outline. Invite learners to read Ecclesiastes 1:12-17 to themselves to learn where the Preacher looked for an answer about the meaning of life and the conclusion to which he came. After several minutes, suggest that learners talk with those sitting near them about their conclusions. Invite some learners to share their conclusions.

Invite learners to scan Ecclesiastes 2:1-11 to answer the question, Can pleasure satisfy? Invite learners to find the kinds of indulgences in which the Preacher sought the answer. Note his conclusion in verse 11.

State that the pleasures mentioned are not essentially evil and that ultimately the Preacher identified the missing part. Call on a learner to read Ecclesiastes 2:24-25 aloud while other learners listen for a different perspective. Call for response. Emphasize that the missing element was that God had no place in the activities. Note that the writer does not yet have the Christian perspective of life but that it is ultimately stated in the teachings of Jesus in Matthew 6:33. Invite learners to turn to the passage. Call on a learner to read it aloud.

Give the Truth a Personal Focus

Share the story "Dead-end street" (*Applying the Lesson*).Ask: What makes life meaningful for you? Recall the discussion with which the study was begun.

---

1. Francisco, *Introducing the Old Testament*, p. 230.

August 5

Times and Seasons

Basic Passage: Ecclesiastes 3

Focal Passage: Ecclesiastes 3:1-15

In an art gallery, the same picture can produce different reactions from different people. One viewer may see a sunrise, another, in the same picture, a sunset. In the opening verses of Ecclesiastes 3, we have a picture of life, a poem of exceptional beauty, but one that has produced a variety of responses. There can be little doubt how it was originally understood, at least by one person, for it produced the despairing exclamation, "What profit hath he that worketh in that wherein he laboureth?" (v. 9). If all of life is arbitrarily determined by God, giving the human creature neither voice nor choice, then the natural reaction is, "What's the use?" But there is another viewpoint expressed in the captivating words, "He hath made every thing beautiful in his time" (v. 11). This glimmer of Godward confidence comes to fruition in the New Testament with its teaching on the Fatherhood of God and all this involves in protection, provision, direction, discipline, and eternal purpose. As Christians, we must draw our own conclusions from this poem written by "the Preacher."

Study Aim: *To recognize the hand of God in all life's experiences and cooperate with His purposes*

STUDYING THE BIBLE

Whatever its perplexities, this Old Testament poem has fascinated a wide range of individuals, including a contemporary songwriter who affirms, "Everything is beautiful in its own way." But all the attention given has done little to correct misunderstanding of these lines. There are still those who read them as a confirmation of William Ernest Henley's proud boast, "I am the master of my fate; I am the captain of my soul." Others take them as a tribute to those who take advantage of life's opportunities, those occasions which "taken at the flood, leads on to fortune." But such surmises are proved wrong by verse 2, "A time to be born, and a time to die." We do not enter this world, or leave it, on our own schedule or by our own planning. The poem as a whole, therefore, is a recognition of God's sovereign control over all of life.

I. Life's Varied Pattern (Eccl. 3:1-8)

Though the rhythm of Hebrew poetry is largely lost in translation, we can still sense the beauty of the Preacher's words. His poem consists of seven couplets in each of which two conflicting actions are described. While they belong to an ancient culture, and reflect its practices, the ideas presented in contrasted statements have parallels in our own experiences. A helpful exercise would be to read these verses in the *Good News Bible* which begins, "Everything that happens in this world happens at the time God chooses."

1 To every thing there is a season, and a time to every purpose under the heaven:

2 A time to be born, and a time to die; a time to plant, and a time to pluck up that which is planted;

3 A time to kill, and a time to heal; a time to break down, and a time to build up;

4 A time to weep, and a time to laugh; a time to mourn, and a time to dance;

5 A time to cast away stones, and a time to gather stones together; a time to embrace, and a time to refrain from embracing;

6 A time to get, and a time to lose; a time to keep, and a time to cast away;

7 A time to rend, and a time to sew; a time to keep silence, and a time to speak;

8 A time to love, and a time to hate; a time of war, and a time of peace.

1. Review.—Verse 2 begins with the start and the conclusion of earthly life, two events that are obviously beyond an individual's control. In the same verse, planting and plucking refer to the activities of seedtime and harvest. Conditions of war are described in verse 3 when killing and healing both take place; also demolishing buildings and restoring them. Verse 4 brings together seasons of sorrow and rejoicing. A field's usefulness could be destroyed by covering it with rocks (v. 5), while their removal could restore that usefulness. The suggestion is offered that the second part of this verse refers, not to the embraces of lovers, but to the Eastern method of greeting. Business activities may be described in verse 6, accumulating property or wealth, and losing these. Eastern practice is again reflected in verse 7. Clothes torn as a sign of mourning or anger need afterward to be repaired. The same circumstances may reduce a person to silence, although this will only be temporary, and normal communication will soon be renewed. For the individual, emotions may alternate between love and hate (v. 8); for the community, between war and peace.

2. Application.—The poet's list covers a great many of the events and activities of life, but is obviously not complete. Neither does it fit our present circumstances at every point, which we may see as a challenge to make our own contribution to these ancient couplets. As examples, we might add: a time to work, and a time to play; a time to save, and a time to spend; a time to wake, and a time to sleep. The almost endless possibilities indicate the great variety of experiences that life affords. We should find cause for gratitude in the changing patterns of every day experience.

II. Fatalism or Faith? (Eccl. 3:9-10)

These next two verses reveal the frustration of this Old Testament poet as he enumerated the routines of life. He could not banish God from his thinking, yet he failed to see any positive pattern in human experience. Though clinging to his belief in God, he fell back on his repeated question, "What's the use?" We will reproduce his words, and then examine the alternatives that faced him and continue to face us.

> **9 What profit hath he that worketh in that wherein he laboureth?**
>
> **10 I have seen the travail, which God hath given to the sons of men to be exercised in it.**

1. The dilemma.—The Revised Standard Version renders these verses, "What gain has the worker from his toil? I have seen the business that God has given to the sons of men to be busy with." All the things recited in verses 2-8 keep people busy. But where do they lead? What satisfactions do they bring? As Christians, we may have difficulty sympathizing with the repeated pessimism and despair of such questions. But can we not commend the writer for asking them? It is by asking questions that we eventually learn, a fact that is nowhere better demonstrated than in the Book of Job whose demand for explanations finally brought a vision of God.

2. The alternatives.—What explanations for the riddle of life were available to the writer of Ecclesiastes, and are still open to us? Which of the following is to be preferred?

a. Fatalism.—Life may be seen as a prison in which people's actions are dictated by a cruel jailer named Fate. He cannot be influenced by compassion or reason, but arbitrarily imposes his will on his victims. Worse than any heathen god, he cannot be appeased by gifts or offerings but distributes favors to some, and mortal blows to others, without rhyme or reason.

b. Superstition.—There are those who would not venture from their beds without consulting their horoscope. They believe that the hour and the date of birth subject them for life to the whims of a distant planet. Astrologers and fortune-tellers are the priests and prophets of this false religion that has dominated the minds of many since biblical times.

c. Humanism.—Always popular, particularly today, is the idea that we can control our own destinies. The progress of technology has created in some the belief that nothing is beyond the achievement of mortal man. Yet the vice, crime, and terrorism abroad in the world seriously challenge the claim to human progress.

d. Godward faith.—Though not strongly expressed in Ecclesiastes, surrender to complete despair is checked again and again by references to the activity of God. The book may contain more questions than answers, but when it turns attention from the uncertainties of life to the fact of the Almighty, it prepares the way for the brighter vision that came in the Lord Jesus Christ and His gospel.

III. Glimpses of Truth (Eccl. 3:11-15)

The name of God appears six times in verses 10-15. It is that name that changes the tone of the Preacher. Though his spiritual vision is limited, he sees enough to kindle hope. As we read his struggling words we are given new reason to give thanks for that revelation of God that came in the person of His Son.

11 He hath made every thing beautiful in his time: also he hath set the world in their heart, so that no man can find out the work that God maketh from the beginning to the end.

12 I know that there is no good in them, but for a man to rejoice, and to do good in his life.

13 And also that every man should eat and drink, and enjoy the good of all his labour, it is the gift of God.

14 I know that, whatsoever God doeth, it shall be for ever: nothing can be put to it, nor any thing taken from it: and God doeth it, that men should fear before him.

15 That which hath been is now; and that which is to be hath already been; and God requireth that which is past.

1. The mystery of God.—Our poet's trouble is that he cannot understand the ways of God. He believes that "he has put eternity into man's mind" (v. 11, RSV), that is, He has given all of us a desire to grasp the unknown, a curiosity to probe into the future, but this desire and curiosity are not satisfied. In thus expressing himself, the poet says nothing new, for the human heart has always cried out for a clearer vision. "Canst thou by searching find out God? canst thou find out the Almighty unto perfection?" (Job 11:7). "O the depths of the riches both of the wisdom and knowledge of God! how unsearchable are his judgments, and his ways past finding out!" (Rom. 11:33). The mystery of His person and the inscrutability of His ways should lead us to worship (v. 14).

2. Finding satisfaction.—A conclusion previously reached is now repeated. "So I realized that all we can do is be happy and do the best we can while we are still alive. All of us should eat and drink and enjoy what we have worked for. It is God's gift" (vv. 12-13, GNB). There is a faint parallel here with Paul's statement, "I have learned, in whatsoever state I am, therewith to be content" (Phil. 4:11). Nothing can be gained by a fretful attitude toward life. To be satisfied with what we have, and acknowledge God as the giver (Eccl. 3:13), is commendable. But the best in life is not gained by a passive acceptance of its circumstances. Paul took higher ground when he said, "For we are labourers together with God" (1 Cor. 3:9). In Jesus Christ, this New Testament man had found meaning and purpose in life. He recognized that God was at work calling out a people for Himself. Paul devoted his life, in time and energy, to working with God toward this goal.

APPLYING THE LESSON

That settles the matter.—A bumper sticker was quite popular a few years ago which said, "God said it, and I believe it, and that settles the matter." In reaction to that another bumper sticker made a statement which even more clearly pronounces the sovereignty of God. This sticker said, "God said it, and that settles the matter, whether I believe it or not." All of life is under the sovereign control of God.

Work your plan.—An old adage suggests: "Plan your work and then work your plan." Thomas Edison exemplified this approach to life. On his fifty-fifth birthday, Thomas Edison attended a party given in his honor. "What plans do you have for the future?" he was asked. "From now until I am 75," Edison said, "I will be occupied with my work. At 75, I intend to learn how to play bridge. At 80, I am going to gossip with the ladies, and at 85, I expect to take up golf." His enthusiastic listener asked, "And at 90? What do you expect to do then?" Edison shrugged his shoulders and said, "I don't know. I never plan more than 30 years in advance!"

Edison discovered the secret espoused by the writer of Ecclesiastes, that there is a purpose for every part of life and every day of life. So he planned his life to make the most out of it.

Unquenched optimism.—As the man drove down the street he noticed some boys playing a Little League ball game in the park, so he stopped to watch. He stood behind one of the dugouts for a few minutes. Finally, he asked one of the boys in the dugout, "What's the score?" The little boy said, "Twenty-one to nothing. We're behind." The visitor said, "You must really feel bad." "Not really," the boy replied, "We haven't even gotten up to bat yet!"

Some can approach life with that unquenched optimism, but many times the load of life is so heavy that we are overwhelmed with the pessimism which permeated the life of the philosopher who wrote Ecclesiastes.

Is this freedom?—The prodigal son in Jesus' story in Luke 15 left home in search of freedom. He thought that freedom was to be found in the far country. Once he was liberated from the bondage of his father, he would be free indeed. He soon discovered that no one is ever completely free. He discovered that giving himself to the desires of his flesh and escaping to the far country was the worst kind of bondage. In the words of Helmut Thielicke: "This is the great new thing that suddenly dawns upon him—him who, after all, set out to be free, free above all from his father. He is bound to his homesickness, so he must amuse himself. He is bound to urges, so he must satisfy them. He is bound to a grand style of living and therefore he cannot let it go. He would be prepared to lie and cheat and disregard every good resolution, so spellbound is he by his standard of living. That's what freedom looks like outside the Father's house—to be bound, to have to do this and that, to be under a spell, to be compelled to pursue the path he has chosen by an inexorable law."[1]

The only kind of freedom worth having is the freedom that comes when a person submits himself to the Master. The Master sets us free from self, free from sin, free from Satan, and enables us to become what we were originally created to be: children of God.

Possessing everything.—A young serviceman stationed in Korea became involved in an orphans' home named Hae Kwang Won, about an hour's drive from the base. He would spend his Saturdays trying to encourage sixty orphans. They had very little in comparison to American children—no store-bought toys, no change of clothing, no meals with meat or milk. Yet, many of the children had a beautiful faith in God.

One day he noticed a Korean Bible which was one of the orphan girl's few possessions. The Bible fell open to show an underlined verse. He could not read Korean but he figured out it was 2 Corinthians 6:10. That evening he looked up the verse and found this beautiful testimony of the little girl's satisfaction with the Lord: "As sorrowful, yet always rejoicing; as poor, yet making many rich; as having nothing, and yet possessing everything" (RSV).

TEACHING THE CLASS

Main Idea: God has set order in the universe and in the experiences of mankind.

Suggested Teaching Aim: Learners will thank God for His order and decide to accept His purposes for that order in their lives.

Introduce the Bible Study

Share the story "That settles the matter" found in *Applying the Lesson*. Display the main idea of the lesson. Point out that this truth stands whether we believe it or act upon it or not.

State that the study for today includes a beautiful and well-known poem from "the Preacher." Invite learners to turn in their

Bibles to Ecclesiastes 3 to find the poem and to learn its implications for their lives.

Search for Biblical Truth

Share the information about how the poem in verses 1-8 is structured. The information is found in the first paragraph of part I titled "Life's Varied Pattern." Call on a learner to read the verses aloud while other learners listen to enjoy the beauty of the peom,

A Teaching Outline

1. Consider the rhyme and purposes of life's experiences.
2. Interpret the Preacher's statements about the order God has set in motion.
3. Praise God for the order of His universe and accept the purpose of that order in our lives.

When the reading is finished, state that the emphasis is on order and on the plan that God built in when He created this universe. Share the story titled "Work your plan" found in *Applying the Lesson*.

Display the following outline as a guide for the study.

ORDER THAT GIVES MEANING

1. Times and Seasons (Eccl. 3:1-8)
   (1) Conflicting Actions
   (2) Order and Meaning
2. Pessimism vs. Optimism (Eccl. 3:9-10)
   (1) The dilemma
   (2) The alternatives
3. The Known and the Unknown (Eccl. 3:11-15)
   (1) The mystery of God: The unknown
   (2) The acceptance of faith: The known

Direct learners to review verses 1-8 to note the conflicting actions. Invite some learners to name some of them. Review some of the information in *Studying the Bible* about these activities in the culture of the writer. Ask: How do these conflicting actions result in order and meaning? Elicit response.

Remind learners that the activities reflect the culture of the times. Direct them to work with persons sitting near them to write some similar statements that reflect activities of today. An example would be: A time to buy and store food, a time to consume food. After several minutes, call for response. Point out that some of the contrasting activities mentioned by the Preacher are universal. For example, A time to weep, and a time to laugh.

Share the story "Unquenched optimism" (*Applying the Lesson*). Call attention to item 2 of the outline. Invite a learner to read verses 9-10 aloud.[1] Use information from *Studying the Bible* to explain the dilemma and the alternatives.

Call attention to item 3 of the outline and invite a learner to read verses 11-15 aloud while other learners listen to be able to identify the known and the unknown. Call for response. Use information from *Studying the Bible* for clarification.

Give the Truth a Personal Focus

Share "Is this freedom?" from *Applying the Lesson*. State that the only true freedom is found in acceptance of the order and purpose of God in both the universe and in our own personal lives.

Share the story "Possessing everything" found in *Applying the Lesson*. Invite learners to join in prayer praising God for His purposes and accepting them for our lives.

1. Helmut Thielicke, *The Waiting Father*, Translated by John W. Doberstein (New York: Harper and Brothers, 1959), p. 25.

August 12

A New Teacher of Wisdom

Basic Passage: Matthew 7

Focal Passage: Matthew 7:13-29

No stronger statement on the authority of the Old and the New Testaments can be found in the Bible than Hebrews 1:1-2. The first affirmation is that "God . . . spake in times past . . . by the prophets." Authority is thus given to Old Testament spokesmen. However, the statement continues to say of this same God that He has "in these last days spoken unto us by his Son." The writer of

Hebrews proceeded to demonstrate the supremacy of the Son over previous messengers, angelic and human. In our recent studies the point has often been made that Old Testament precepts and pronouncements must be made subject to a New Testament test. The fullness of divine revelation came in the person and teaching of the Lord Jesus Christ who is described as "the power of God, and the wisdom of God" (1 Cor. 1:24). The ultimate voice of wisdom is the voice of Jesus Christ, whose teachings are preserved for us in the Gospels and interpreted to us in the Epistles. Very suitably, therefore, we conclude this series with a lesson from the Sermon on the Mount and two excerpts from the writings of James.

Study Aim: *To give heed to the words of the greatest teacher, Jesus, the Son of God*

STUDYING THE BIBLE

The Sermon on the Mount (Matt. 5—7) is a collection of the teachings of Jesus on Christian discipleship. There is a shorter version in Luke 6:10-49 which is valuable because it enables us to set the scene of this teaching. Jesus had chosen His disciples (v. 13) and performed miracles of healing (vv. 17-19), after which "he lifted up his eyes on his disciples, and said . . ." (v. 20). We turn to Matthew's account for its more detailed reporting of some of the things He said.

I. Choose the Right Way (Matt. 7:13-14)

The idea of life as a road, with responsibility resting on each individual to be sure that he travels the right road, is common in religious literature. In his classic *The Pilgrim's Progress,* Bunyan began with a choice of ways: that which led to the City of Destruction, or that which reached its terminus in the Celestial City. An Old Testament counterpart to our Lord's urgent teaching may be found in Proverbs 4:14-19 (see lesson for July 11). There the choice is between "the way of the wicked" and "the path of the just." These are Jesus' words:

> **13 Enter ye in at the strait gate: for wide is the gate, and broad is the way, that leadeth to destruction, and many there be which go in thereat:**
>
> **14 Because strait is the gate, and narrow is the way, which leadeth unto life, and few there be that find it.**

The archaic word "strait," meaning narrow, or restricted, has survived in geographical terms, for example, the Strait of

Gibraltar, a narrow stretch of water leading into the Mediterranean Sea. Jesus was acknowledging that the highway to life has no outward glamor, in contrast to the road to destruction which has plenty of eye appeal. The devil knows how to entice people to walk with him. As a result, Jesus said, few choose the right way and many follow the wrong. Wisdom is not always with the majority. The big difference between the statement in Proverbs and these words from the Sermon on the Mount is the speaker. Jesus not only offered advice, but His own personal help, for He said, "I am the way. . . . no man cometh unto the Father but by me" (John 14:6).

II. Embrace True Teaching (Matt. 7:15-20)

There are more reasons than one why people miss the right road and commit themselves to the wrong, though Satan is behind them all. One of his ruses is not to steer away from religion, but to seduce the unwary with false religion. As with the broad way that leads to destruction, untruth dresses itself up to look attractive and so deceive its victims. The agents of heresy are wolves at heart, but make themselves appear as sheep.

15 Beware of false prophets, which come to you in sheep's clothing, but inwardly they are ravening wolves.

16 Ye shall know them by their fruits. Do men gather grapes of thorns, or figs of thistles?

17 Even so every good tree bringeth forth good fruit; but a corrupt tree bringeth forth evil fruit.

18 A good tree cannot bring forth evil fruit, neither can a corrupt tree bring forth good fruit.

19 Every tree that bringeth not forth good fruit is hewn down, and cast into the fire.

20 Wherefore by their fruits ye shall know them.

It is unlikely that Jesus was referring to Pharisees or Sadducees, though at other times He warned his followers against these groups. Pharisees taught salvation through works, and Sadducees denied the resurrection. But by "false prophets" our Lord was probably describing heretical teachers who would infiltrate the church. In recording our Lord's words, Matthew undoubtedly saw their relevance for Christians of the second half of the first century. By then, a variety of unscriptural ideas were in circulation as, for example, gnosticism against which the apostle John wrote so strongly. With this teaching, the deity of our Lord was the issue. It denied that He is God's eternal Son. Frank Stagg thinks that the appearance of the word "evildoers" (v. 23, RSV), or lawless ones, furnishes a clue.[1] The apostle Paul rebuked these when he asked, "Shall we continue in sin, that grace may abound?" (Rom. 6:1), for they taught that Christians, being freed from the law, were also free of all restraint.

III. Practice Sincere Discipleship (Matt. 7:21-23)

False prophets were adept in the use of words, but Jesus said that more important than what they said was how they behaved. They should be judged by their "fruit." Character is the test of sincerity and genuineness.

21 Not every one that saith unto me, Lord, Lord, shall enter into the kingdom of heaven; but he that doeth the will of my Father which is in heaven.

22 Many will say to me in that day, Lord, Lord, have we not prophesied in thy name? and in thy name have cast out devils? and in thy name done many wonderful works?

23 And then will I profess unto them, I never knew you: depart from me, ye that work iniquity.

The apostle James wrote words that must have astonished many who first read them. To be "masters" (KJV), or "teachers" (RSV), in the church was considered a worthy ambition. But this apostle said, "Let not many of you become teachers, my brethren, for you know that we who teach shall be judged with greater strictness" (Jas. 3:1, RSV). He was warning against ambition that pays little heed to the qualifications for, and responsibilities of, service in the church. James was doubtless familiar with the serious words of the Lord Jesus in Matthew 7. In His days on earth, Jesus had followers whose pious professions were not evidence of try loyalty, but a cover-up for insincerity. These people even preached and worked miracles in His name; but He disowned them. In our time, Christianity has been repeatedly disgraced by persons in the public eye whose behavior was in conflict with their preaching. All of us, whether we hold office or not, need to keep our conduct in line with our creed.

IV. Build on Strong Foundations (Matt. 7:24-27)

Luke's account of the Sermon on the Mount also concludes with this parable (Luke 6:47-49). The most significant difference in the two accounts is that Luke says that the man who built wisely "digged deep" in order to secure a strong foundation. However, to read both accounts is to realize that the two houses were similar in construction and appearance. The emphasis, in fact, is not on the houses but their foundations, one rock and the other sand. Both may have been built in a flood plain, for even to this day there is sometimes need to build where flooding is possible. The builder of the second house, however, took no steps to protect himself against disaster. The result was complete destruction. Jesus compared him to "everyone that heareth these sayings of mine, and doeth them not."

> **24 Therefore whosoever heareth these sayings of mine, and doeth them, I will liken him unto a wise man, which built his house upon a rock:**
> **25 And the rain descended, and the floods came, and the winds blew, and beat upon that house; and it fell not: for it was founded upon a rock.**
> **26 And every one that heareth these sayings of mine, and doeth them not, shall be liked unto a foolish man, which built his house upon the sand:**
> **27 And the rain descended, and the floods came, and the winds blew, and beat upon that house; and it fell: and great was the fall of it.**

According to this parable, survival in the storms of life depends on whether we are hearers and doers of Christ's teaching, or hearers only. Jesus did not indicate the nature of the storms, but by the time Matthew wrote his Gospel, Christians were being subject to persecution and the quality of their faith was being tested. The strength of our spiritual foundations can be strained by a number of things—physical health, finances, family situations, and even church disputes.

V. Teaching that Impressed (Matt. 7:28-29)

Those who listened to our Lord's teaching consisted of the disciples, for whom it was originally intended, and "the people" (v. 28). The presence of multitudes is mentioned in 5:1. Apparently, as Jesus continued His teaching, the crowd closed in on Him, fascinated by what He was saying. According to the following verses, there were two reactions. The first was to the content of His teaching. In the parable of the two houses, for example, human destiny was made to depend on response to His teaching. In verses 21-23 He said that He would pass judgment, separating the bogus and the real, when the kingdom of heaven comes to fulfillment. Earlier in the Sermon on the Mount, He several times quoted from the Old Testament, and after adding, "But I say unto you," made ancient laws more demanding than traditionally understood. Thus He made himself greater than Moses (Heb. 3:3-6).

28 And it came to pass, when Jesus had ended these sayings, the people were astonished at his doctrine:
29 For he taught them as one having authority, and not as the scribes.

The second reaction was to the style of His teaching. They were accustomed to the ways of the scribes, who were originally copiers of the law, but progressed to being its interpreters. They merely echoed the positions taken by rabbis and strictly adhered to accepted traditions. There was an independence and freshness about the style of our Lord that astonished them. He respected the past, but was not enslaved to it. He upheld the ancient Scriptures, but did not hesitate to modify them, never reducing their authority, but always sharpening it. Every time He said, "But I say unto you," He raised the law to an even higher standard as He demanded higher standards from His followers. "Think not that I am come to destroy the law, or the prophets," he said; "I am not come to destroy, but to fulfil" (Matt. 5:17).

APPLYING THE LESSON

The lessons of sacrifice.—No one has written more effectively on discipleship and sacrifice than Richard J. Foster. In one of his books, he describes the renunciations of the monks. A prime example was Anthony, "the father of the monks" who lived in the second and third centuries. At the age of eighteen, he gave away all of his inherited land, sold all of his possessions, and retreated into the desert where for twenty years he lived in complete solitude. When he emerged from the solitude of the desert, he was marked with graciousness and love and kindness. He carried on an effective ministry for many years until, in his final years, he retreated into the desert again and died at the age of 105.

Many excesses marked the monasticism of these early monks, but Foster points out some lessons they learned. They renounced possessions in order to learn the kind of detachment which frees us from the control of others. They renounced speech in order to learn the kind of love which frees us from the need to control others. They renounced activity in order to learn prayer which frees us to be controlled by God.

The way of the devil.—The devil does not come to us in a red suit, horns, and a pitchfork in hand. Rather, he comes to us under clever disguises in his attempts to lead us down the road of destruction.

Jerry Gunnells captured the spirit of Satan's approach when he said, "The devil searches out our basic character flaws and comes with a design to ruin us. To the sensual man, he comes in skirts. To the bold man, he bids him live by nerve, sensation, and instinct. To the timid man, he speaks about quietly withdrawing and playing it safe. To the intelligent man, he tantalizes with the prospect of knowing good and evil. To the lazy man the devil whispers 'tomorrow.' When the devil makes his move, you may be certain that it will have stature, boldness, and imagination."[2]

Not practicing what they preached.—A survey of women attending a meeting to protest "deceptive packaging" revealed that 15 percent of them tinted their hair, 22 percent of them wore false eyelashes, 25 percent wore eyeshadow, 39 percent wore wigs, 80 percent wore rouge, 93 percent wore nail polish, 98 percent were lipstick, and all 100 percent of them voted strongly in favor of a resolution condemning any kind of false packaging!

How often we in the church do the same thing. We fail to practice in our lives what we proclaim with our lips. We wear the label "Christian" but then do not live like a Christian.

Foundation of faith.—One of the most fascinating personalities in all of Christian history was the man George Muller. Pastor, philanthropist, preacher—George Muller made great accomplishments because of his faith and his commitment to prayer. He was involved in various forms of mission work but is remembered most for his orphanage in Bristol. He renounced a regular salary and refused throughout the rest of his life to make any requests for financial support either for himself or for his philanthropic projects. He depended entirely on prayer and the provisions of God.

His biographer cites four spiritual laws which with growing power controlled the life of George Muller: "His supreme aim was the glory of God; his sole resort, believing prayer; his one trusted oracle, the inspired Word; his one divine Teacher, the Holy Spirit."[3] Those spiritual principles provided an unshakable foundation which held firm through all the ups and downs of his ministry.

A good teacher.—Sometimes we can recognize the goodness of something only by contrasting it to that which is bad. In other words, you may not recognize how delicious the pie is that your mother made until you taste a number of other pies that don't quite measure up. Likewise, the superiority of Jesus' teaching became clear when His listeners compared it to the kind of teaching they were used to hearing. Someone has said, "The only bad teaching is the teaching which leaves the listener completely uninterested, completely indifferent, unmoved to learn and unstimulated to think."

TEACHING THE CLASS

Main Idea: God looks at the inner person, not only on the outward form of a follower.

Suggested Teaching Aim: Learners will assess their own attitudes and behaviors to determine whether they are on the way of life in Christ.

Introduce the Bible Study

Ask: If you stopped people on the street and asked them how they can tell if someone is a Christian, what are some of the responses you would expect to get? Elicit response. Continue by asking: In what ways, if any, would you expect church members to answer differently? Elicit response. Ask: Do you think God determines whether someone is a believer by these sames indicators? If not, what are his considerations? Why do discrepancies exist in the way we measure Christianity and the way God measures Christianity?

Point out that the study for today will help us to define accurately how God determines if we are following "the way of life." Note that we turn to study the New Testament with this lesson and particularly the Sermon on the Mount. Invite learners to open their Bibles to Matthew 7.

Search for Biblical Truth

Use information from *Studying the Bible* to provide the background setting of these teachings of Jesus.

Call on a learner to read Matthew 7:13-14 aloud while other learners listen for Jesus' description of "the way of life." Call for response. Share the story "The lessons of sacrifice" found in *Applying the Lesson.*

A Teaching Outline

1. Determine "the way of life" as taught by Jesus.
2. Renew commitment to truly following Jesus in the way He taught.

Ask: In your experience, is following Jesus presented as a life of sacrifice in today's teaching and preaching? Why or why not? Contrast these teachings of Jesus with common approaches of presenting Christianity today.

Share the story "The way of the devil" (*Applying the Lesson*). Call on a learner to read verses 15-20 aloud. Share information from *Studying the Bible* about the need for this warning.

Ask: What evidence do you see of heretical teachers in the church today? How can you tell the true teachers of God's way and the false prophets? (By their fruit, their behavior.)

State that Jesus went beyond the overt behavior in giving guidance about false teachers. Call on a learner to read verses 21-23 aloud while other learners listen for further tests of whether a follower is genuine or not. Call for response.

Share "Not practicing what they preached" (*Applying the Lesson*). Ask: Do you think the women in this survey would have seen the discrepancy in their attitudes? How would they have explained their behavior? Elicit response.

Continue by asking: Do you think false prophets easily see the discrepancy in their attitudes? Why? Elicit response. Continue: Is it possible that we too have major discrepancies from the teachings of Jesus that we do not see? Is it possible that we may think that we follow Him when we don't? If so, how can we be certain that we are on the narrow road that leads to life?

State that Jesus said that it depends on the foundation on which we build. Call on a learner to read verses 24-27 aloud. When the reading is finished, ask: What is the foundation that will stand when the storm comes? (Being both hearers and doers of Christ's teachings.) Note that both builders in the parable built where floods come, that is, both would experience testing. The foundation made the difference.

Point out that both the content and the style of these teachings of Jesus amazed His listeners. Call on a learner to read verses 28-29 aloud.

Give the Truth a Personal Focus

Invite learners on the basis of the personal assessment of their attitudes and behaviors during this study to renew their commitment to follow Jesus.

---

1. Frank Stagg, *The Broadman Bible Commentary,* Volume 8 (Nashville: Broadman Press, 1969), p. 122.
2. "The Doctrine of Condemnation," a sermon by Jerry Gunnells preached at Springhill Baptist Church, Mobile, AL, May 10, 1981.
3. Basil Miller, *George Muller* (Minneapolis: Dimension Books, 1941), p. 83.

August 19

Who Is Wise?

Basic Passages: James 1:1-8; 3:1 to 4:12

Focal Passages: James 1:1-8; 3:13-18

Having spent some time recently in the Old Testament Book of Proverbs, we will recognize similarities between that book and the Epistle of James. For one thing, both discuss at length the subject of wisdom, and both do this in a disjointed style that shows little or no organization. Expository writers who have tried to outline this short epistle have ended up with as many as twenty-five different sections. This feature, rather than detracting from the appeal of the book, adds to it. James was concerned for the practical application of the message of the gospel. He wrote to and for people who were paying little heed to the behavioral side of Christianity. Hence, he exhorted them to be "doers of the word" (1:22), thus echoing, not only the Wisdom teachers of the Old Testament, but also the teaching of the Sermon on the Mount. He did not wear his readers out with long discussions, but held their attention by making his individual messages short and to the point. Maybe we can learn from this.

Study Aim: *To consider the subject of Wisdom in the setting of Christian discipleship*

STUDYING THE BIBLE

Following custom, the writer of this epistle began with his name, James. He was obviously well known in the churches since he added no further identification than to describe himself as "a servant," or slave, "of the Lord Jesus Christ." The opinion is strongly held that this James was none other than the half-brother of Jesus (Gal. 1:19). He became leader of the church in Jerusalem (Acts 21:17-18), comprised of Jewish converts, and probably addressed his Epistle to fellow Jews, "scattered abroad" in the Gentile world. What he wrote quickly led to the subject of wisdom which, we need to remind ourselves, does not mean book knowledge, but that gift from God that enables us to live in accordance with His will.

I. Right Attitude Toward Trials (Jas. 1:1-4)

Without exception, New Testament Epistles were addressed to people who knew what it was to suffer. They had their share of the hardships borne by everybody, but added to these were the persecutions they endured because of their faith. James wrote about "divers temptations" (v. 2), "various trials" (RSV), a phrase broad enough to include all these adverse experiences. He was concerned over how his readers reacted to life's unwelcome happenings.

1 James, a servant of God and of the Lord Jesus Christ, to the twelve tribes which are scattered abroad, greeting.

2 My brethren, count it all joy when ye fall into divers temptations;

3 Knowing this, that the trying of your faith worketh patience,

4 But let patience have her perfect work, that ye may be perfect and entire, wanting nothing.

1. Joy in adversity (v. 2).—James was not suggesting that, because they were Christians, his readers should enjoy pain. When they stubbed a toe, it hurt them just as it did everybody else, and they were likely to exclaim, "Ouch!" But, when troubles come, Christians should not indulge in self-pity, but recognize that both body aches and heartaches can be productive of good. Possessed of this attitude, they can rejoice even when circumstances seem against them, being confident that God can bring blessing out of the worst situation.

2. Benefit from trials (vv. 3-4).—This teaching was not intended to produce a "grit your teeth and bear it" attitude. James presumed on the faith of his readers and knew that when faith is possessed and exercised it can produce "steadfastness" (RSV). We stand firm against the buffetings of life, and by so doing achieve spiritual maturity, "perfect and entire."

II. Source of Needed Wisdom (Jas. 1:5-8)

That James was not claiming absolute spiritual perfection as a result of patient endurance is made clear by these verses. Those who would be "wanting nothing" in steadfastness of character might nevertheless be aware of a lack of wisdom. The very trials they had been through could reveal this inadequacy. Though achieving self-discipline, they could very well come short in their attitudes toward others, a fault that could only be corrected by a bestowment of divine wisdom.

5 If any of you lack wisdom, let him ask of God, that giveth to all men liberally, and upbraideth not; and it shall be given him.

6 But let him ask in faith, nothing wavering. For he that wavereth is like a wave of the sea driven with the wind and tossed.

7 For let not that man think that he shall receive any thing of the Lord.

8 A double-minded man is unstable in all his ways.

1. Asking for wisdom (v. 5).—A sure test of the measure of wisdom we possess is our reaction to adversity. The nature of this wisdom is strikingly indicated by James's exhortation to those who lack it, "let him ask of God." For certain kinds of wisdom we turn to books or experts, teachers and professors. But there is only one source of biblical wisdom, God Himself. The psalmist said, "I will run in the way of thy commandments when thou enlargest my understanding!" (119:32, RSV). Earthly teachers sometimes make the mistake of scolding pupils who own up to their inadequacies. Not so God. As our compassionate Heavenly Father, he gives without reproof, and He does this "liberally."

2. Asking in faith (vv. 6-8).—By faith we are to understand implicit trust in God. James was nothing if not emphatic. He made the good point that prayer is invalid unless it is made with full confidence in the ability and willingness of God to answer. To be a doubter is to be "double-minded," shifting constantly from belief to unbelief, or, at best, halfhearted belief. Of a person so described, James said that he "is unstable in all his ways." His prayer life is ineffective, hence his entire life-style is erratic. A firm trust in God is necessary for the development of Christian character and the maintenance of Christian standards.

III. How Wisdom Proves Itself (Jas. 3:13-18)

We pass over verses to which we will return in the next lesson. Chapter 3 begins with the exhortation, "My brethren, be not many masters, knowing that we shall receive the greater condemnation" (3:1). We have already noted that James was addressing himself to persons who aspired to be teachers, a function that was held in high esteem. We recall that, during His ministry, our Lord was invited to speak at synagogue services (Mark 1:39; Luke 6:6). The same practice carried over into Christian worship services, and some people coveted this recognition for themselves, qualified or not. James was clearly disturbed over the complications that resulted, and he called on all aspirants to the teaching task to count the cost. Persons in leadership positions, he said, will be held responsible for their actions to a higher degree than others. From this point, he went on to describe how people get into trouble through not controlling their tongues. His powerful words have application to all Christians, but specially to those who attempt to teach others. He had these also in mind when he used the phrase "wise man" in verse 13.

> **13 Who is a wise man and endued with knowledge among you? let him shew out of a good conversation his works with meekness of wisdom.**
> **14 But if ye have bitter envying and strife in your hearts, glory not, and lie not against the truth.**
> **15 This wisdom descendeth not from above, but is earthly, sensual, devilish.**
> **16 For where envying and strife is, there is confusion and every evil work.**
> **17 But the wisdom that is from above is first pure, then peaceable, gentle, and easy to be entreated, full of mercy and good fruits, without partiality, and without hypocrisy.**
> **18 And the fruit of righteousness is sown in peace of them that make peace.**

1. True wisdom expressed (v. 13).—We are left to assume that among those to whom James addressed his letter were persons who bragged about their qualifications as teachers. "Let me tell you how to test such people," wrote the apostle. Mere talk is not enough. Their manner of life must be good, in the highest sense. Their wisdom will be expressed in meekness, that is, in an absence of pride and self-assertiveness. Since James has had so much to say about the tongue and talk (vv. 2-12), we might assume that "conversation" (v. 13) is in that context. But here, as elsewhere in the King James Version of the New Testament, this word covers more than what a person says. It describes one's total life-style. The true wise man, or teacher, is not only smart intellectually but has integrity spiritually. He has been a good student in the school of Christ, and has developed likeness to the greatest of teachers, who said, "Blessed are the meek" (Matt. 5:5).

2. False wisdom denounced (vv. 14-16).—Unhealthy ambitions toward leadership positions in the churches were expressing themselves in envy and contentiousness. It is distressing to know that so early in the Christian movement these divisive forces were at work. The devil did his utmost from the beginning to prevent the progress of the gospel. Fortunately, he did not succeed. But who knows what damage has been done, and is still being done, by those who spread discord among the people of God? James said three things about this "bitter jealousy and selfish ambition" (v. 14, RSV). First, it is "earthly," that is, as distinct from heavenly. It is an expression of worldliness, from which Christians should have been delivered. Those who are guilty in these respects behave like unregenerate persons, not those who have been born from above. This is the point made by James's second word, "sensual" or "unspiritual" (RSV). The severest judgment is in the third word, "devilish," a word found only here in the New Testament. Those who sow enmity among Christians are doing Satan's work.

3. God's gift of wisdom (vv. 17-18).—Three characteristics of false wisdom are counterbalanced by seven marks of true wisdom. First among these is *purity of life,* not only abstention from sexual immorality, though that is included, but also the avoidance of all sins. As wisdom itself comes from God, so ability to live on this high plain is God's gift. Then comes *peaceableness,* in sharp contrast to the jealousy and contention that unbridled ambition was producing. *Gentleness,* expressed in consideration of others, also makes a person "open to reason" (RSV). The arrogance of a self-opinionated person prevents him from yielding to contrary ideas and opinions. He stands pat on what he believes and will tolerate no disagreement. Unlike him, the truly "wise man" is "full of mercy and good fruits," that is, he is compassionate and forgiving and shares freely of the benefits he enjoys. Finally, "without partiality" means "unwavering" (see 1:6). His word is not yes today and no tomorrow. And he is "without hypocrisy," or "make believe," a genuine person who makes no attempt at deception. Such an individual is an influence for peace in all his contacts (v. 18).

APPLYING THE LESSON

The difference between knowing and doing.—A reporter visited Mark Twain's haunts in Hannibal, Missouri, some years back in order to gather material for an in-depth profile of Mark Twain. He found one crony who had grown up with Mark Twain. The old friend discounted the glory and fame of his former companion. "Shucks," he said, "I knew as many stories as Sam Clemens. He just writ them down."

That's the difference between knowing and doing. Many people know what to do as Christians. They know how they are to live, they know what God wants them to do—they just don't do it. The thrust of James's Epistle is to get us to be not just hearers and knowers of the Word but doers of the Word.

What God can make out of a wreck.—The Coventry Cathedral in England was bombed repeatedly during World War II. Following the war, money and materials came from all over the world to rebuild it. The old, ruined Cathedral was left as a fore court to the new Cathedral. It was a beautiful edifice built to glorify God. No part of the Cathedral was more impressive than a bust of Christ, situated on one side of the cathedral. The head of Christ was created by an American artist, using only the metal from a wrecked car.

What a picture of the transforming power of Christ. He can take our lives, wrecked by the trials and tragedies of life, and He can mold us into His own image.

Where we go for help.—A missionary, deep in the jungle, came upon a village where a native was pounding heavily on a drum. "What is going on?" inquired the missionary. The native responded, "We have no water." "I see," said the missionary, "so you're praying for rain." "No," the medicine man replied, "I'm sending for the plumber."

At times, we do need to send for plumbers to help us with our water supply and doctors to help us with our sickness and lawyers to help us with our legal problems. However, in the ultimate matters of life, human wisdom will not suffice. In matters of life and death and purpose and power and forgiveness and guidance we can find help only in God through prayer.

Getting smaller all the time.—A father and his little boy walked down a street in Chicago past the place where a skyscraper was being constructed. Glancing up they saw the men at work on a high story of the building. "Father," said the little boy, "what are those little boys doing up there?" "Those are not little boys," he answered, "They are grown men." "Then why do they look so small?" queried the young lad. "Because they are so high," his father answered. After a short pause, the little boy said, "Then Father, when they get all the way up to heaven, there won't be anything left of them, will there?"

What a delightful picture the little boy painted! The closer we get to God, the closer we get to heaven, the smaller we will be. Those who are closest to the Lord do not think little of themselves. They just don't think of themselves. Their focus is on the Lord.

How to deal with envy.—Dr. Gary Collins, who has written wisely on the emotions of human life, gives this advice on how to deal with envy.

First, we need to understand the basic nature of envy. Envy derives from a feeling of inferiority. Understanding the source of envy will challenge us to find those areas in our life in which we can achieve something worthwhile.

Second, we need to recognize its prevalence. Envy is a universal attitude. Therefore, instead of feeling sorry for ourselves when we experience envy, we need to remind ourselves that this is a part of life that all of us have to deal with.

Third, we need to rely on divine strength to help us overcome our envy. In our own strength, envy is difficult to overcome, but with God all things are possible.

Fourth, we need to accept the sovereignty and wisdom of God. God is an all-knowing and all powerful God who gives to us the abilities, responsibilities, and position in life that He wants us to have. When we realize He knows what is best for us, then we can accept who we are and what we are.[1]

TEACHING THE CLASS

Main Idea: Wisdom can grow out of adversity. Adversity is a sure measure of wisdom.

Suggested Teaching Aim: Learners will be able to state the relationship of wisdom and adversity and, therefore, identify appropriate ways to react to adversity.

Introduce the Bible Study

Ask: What is the worst thing that ever happened to you or to someone you know? Elicit response that reflects the adversity common to most of our lives.

Ask in jest: What is the wisest thought you think you ever had? Continue by asking: What is something that you consider yourself wiser about than you used to be? Elicit response.

A Teaching Outline

1. Ponder the relationship of wisdom and adversity.
2. Identify the teachings given by James on adversity and wisdom.
3. State the relationship between wisdom and adversity.
4. Identify appropriate personal attitudes and responses to adversity.

Ask: Is there any relationship between adversities that we experience and the development of wisdom to live by? If so, what is that relationship? How does it work? Elicit response.

State that the study for today will help us to see even more clearly the relationship between adversity and wisdom. Continue by stating that the purpose of the study is to help us to learn how to deal with adversity in appropriate ways. Invite learners to open their Bibles to James.

Search for Biblical Truth

Use information from *Studying the Bible* to provide background material. Note the similarity in style of the Book of James and the Book of Proverbs. Note also that James was concerned for the practical application of the teachings of Christ to daily living. Display the following outline to guide the Bible study.

ADVERSITY AND WISDOM: A COMPATIBLE PAIR

1. Adversity: How to Handle It (Jas. 1:1-4)
2. Wisdom: Its Source and How to Get It (Jas. 1:1-5)
3. Wisdom: What It Looks Like (Jas. 3:13-18)

Share the story "The difference between knowing and doing" found in *Applying the Lesson*. State that this is the difference among Christians that James deals with.

Call attention to item 1 of the outline. Invite learners to read James 1:1-4 to themselves to discover James's instructions for handling adversity. Call for response.

To clarify the teaching and elicit response from learners, ask questions like the following: How can anyone be joyful when one has problems (various trials, v. 2)? Do Christians have to grit their teeth and bear it, that is, develop a holy martyr syndrome? Use information from *Studying the Bible* to help with answers to the questions.

Share the story "Where we go for help" from *Applying the Lesson*. Call attention to item 2 of the outline. Invite a learner to read verses 5-8 aloud while other learners listen for James's counsel about where to go for help. Call for response. Share information from *Studying the Bible* about asking in faith. Share "What God can make out of a wreck" found in *Applying the Lesson*. Call attention to the fact that the comments about adversity and about getting wisdom follow each other. Ask: What is the relationship between wisdom and adversity suggested here?

Call attention to item 3 on the outline. State that verses 13-18 give some indication of what wisdom in a person looks like. Invite learners to read the verses to themselves and be ready to respond. When finished, ask: How does wisdom act in adversity? Elicit response.

Give the Truth a Personal Focus

Invite learners to recall adversities mentioned as the study was begun. Ask: With this teaching from James, what are some appropriate responses in such situations?

---

1. Gary R. Collins, *Overcoming Anxiety* (Santa Ana, Calif.: Visia House Publishers, 1973), pp. 114-15.

August 26

Hearing and Doing

Basic Passage: James 1:22 to 2:26

Focal Passage: James 1:22 to 2:8

There have been wise men who have shut themselves off from the rest of the world, spending their years in contemplation and study. After their deaths, their writings may have made some contribution to human society in the form of speculations and philosophies; but in life they were hermits, separated from the currents of life. We have been studying a kind of wisdom far different from that of the recluse and the monastic. Biblical wisdom, which is in reality divine wisdom, imparts to those who possess it skills for living in the everyday world, with conduct appropriate toward God and others. This practical wisdom is described in both Old and New Testaments, but nowhere more helpfully than in the teaching and example of our Lord. James was late in entering discipleship, probably not until after the resurrection of Jesus (1 Cor. 15:7). But, as Jesus' half brother, growing up with Him in the Nazareth home, he had ample opportunity to know the spirit that Jesus evidenced toward all kinds of people. He made use of the knowledge in the letter that he wrote.

Study Aim: *To cease to be "hearers only" and become "doers of the word"*

STUDYING THE BIBLE

James was a man with pastoral experience. There is New Testament evidence that he was leader of the church in Jerusalem at the time that Paul was exercising his ministry as Christ's messenger to the Gentiles. He came to know people, particularly professing Christian people, and did not hesitate to expose and challenge their weaknesses and faults. He made reference to those who "lack wisdom" (1:5), and showed how this lack expressed itself in personal religion and social relationships. To James, faith was important. But so were what he called "works."

I. Two Kinds of Listeners (Jas. 1:22-25)

In his letter, James had just made some tremendous statements. For example, "Blessed is the man that endureth temptation: for when he is tried, he shall receive the crown of life" (v. 12). And, "Every good gift and every perfect gift is from above, and cometh down from the Father of lights" (v. 17). These are the kind of things that people like to hear. But does our response stop at hearing, or does it lead to doing? James insisted that it should.

22 But be ye doers of the word, and not hearers only, deceiving your own selves.

23 For if any be a hearer of the word, and not a doer, he is like unto a man beholding his natural face in a glass:

24 For he beholdeth himself, and goeth his way, and straightway forgetteth what manner of man he was,

25 But whoso looketh into the perfect law of liberty, and continueth therein, he being not a forgetful hearer, but a doer of the work, this man shall be blessed in his deed.

1. Hearers should be doers (v. 22).—Let us not forget that James was addressing himself to Christians, probably Jewish Christians. A few verses further on, he would use the word *synagogue,* or "assembly" (KJV). A synagogue was a place where the Scriptures were read and expounded. So, whether used in a Christian or a Jewish sense, *synagogue* described a place where listeners were gathered. Our word *auditorium* has the same meaning. So the question may be asked of us, as of James's first-century readers, Does our attendance at church occasions make us listeners only, nothing more? Listening, James insisted, must lead to doing. There must be active response to what we hear. If not, then we are self-deceived, misleading ourselves with the thought that by mere attendance at God's house we are doing our Christian duty.

2. Glancing in a mirror (vv. 23-24).—Mirrors were expensive in New Testament days, and therefore rare. They were made of highly polished metal and would normally only be seen in wealthy homes. A visitor to such a home might get a glimpse of himself, but the experience would be brief, and the impression soon lost. A few minutes later, out on the street, the visitor would not be able to recall how he looked in that mirror. This, James said, is like too many people who look into the mirror of God's Word. The effect is not lasting.

3. Looking and learning (v. 25).—The mirror served as an illustration. But James made clear that he was really referring to "the perfect law of liberty." His Jewish readers would know exactly what is meant by "the law." But by adding "of liberty" James made plain that he was not meaning the ancient Mosaic law, but the new law enshrined in the gospel by which we find freedom to meet God's righteous demands while also being set free from the fear of transgression. If we continue in the gospel, that is, if we allow its teaching constantly to occupy our minds and hearts, we become doers, and enjoy the blessings of those whose daily walk conforms to the divinely given pattern.

II. Two Kinds of Conduct (Jas. 1:26-27)

What understanding about life will come to the person who continues in the teaching of the gospel? James had a way of concentrating his answers down to single examples. He could have elaborated at length, but satisfies himself with a "for instance," as in these verses.

> **26 If any man among you seem to be religious, and bridleth not his tongue, but deceiveth his own heart, this man's religion is vain.**
> **27 Pure religion and undefiled before God and the Father is this, To visit the fatherless and widows in their affliction, and to keep himself unspotted from the world.**

1. Self-control (vv. 26-27*c*).—There is a sharp point in "seem to be religious." Unfortunately, there are many in Christian circles who deserve to have this question mark placed against their names. To all appearances, they are worthy members of the fellowship. They attend worship services, take part in church programs, tithe, support the missionary enterprise—go through all the motions, in fact, of being good Christians. But James put his finger on one flaw, an unbridled tongue. Like a horse that is out of control, their talk lashes out in all directions, causing serious harm to individuals and the fellowship at large. Since James had much to say about undisciplined talk, the conclusion is that this was a major problem in the congregations to which he wrote. The damage that was being done by gossip and false accusation led him to ask believers to judge themselves at this one point. He gave control of the tongue priority over "keep himself unspotted from the world," though he made this his concluding demand.

2. Self-denial (v. 27).—Old Testament laws protected orphans and widows, who were considered to be under the protection of God. "The Lord preserveth the strangers; he relieveth the fatherless and widow" (Ps. 146:9). One of the first actions of the New Testament church was to make provision for widows (Acts 6:1-4). Whether this type of compassion had been neglected by the time James wrote, we cannot tell, but in this verse he made ministry to orphans and widows an evidence of "pure religion," that is, genuine, and with no alloy of selfishness. His word visit meant more than paying a courtesy call. Orphans and widows were often very needy people and it was a Christian's duty to respond to their needs.

III. Two Kinds of People (Jas. 2:1-9,14-17)

With characteristic bluntness, James said that those who profess faith in the Lord Jesus Christ should not at the same time show prejudice toward certain persons. We cannot fail to be impressed by the respect that this member of the Nazareth household showed toward Jesus. Here, by strict interpretation, he referred to Him as "the Lord of glory" (v. 1), a term used for the Shekinah glory of Jehovah. To quote the Fourth Gospel, "We beheld his glory, the glory as of the only begotten of the Father" (John 1:14). Though possessed of such heavenly splendor, the divine son became poor for our sakes, and ministered on earth to the afflicted and deprived. Should not His followers do the same? Unfortunately, James had reason to suspect that Christian congregations were guilty of discrimination.

1 My brethren, have not the faith of our Lord Jesus Christ, the Lord of glory, with respect of persons.

2 For if there come unto your assembly a man with a gold ring, in goodly apparel, and there come in also a poor man in vile raiment;

3 And ye have respect to him that weareth the gay clothing, and say unto him, Sit thou here in a good place; and say to the poor, Stand thou there, or sit here under my footstool:

4 Are ye not then partial in yourselves, and are become judges of evil thoughts?

5 Hearken, my beloved brethren, Hath not God chosen the poor of this world rich in faith, and heirs of the kingdom which he hath promised to them that love him?

6 But ye have despised the poor. Do not rich men oppress you, and draw you before the judgment seats?

7 Do not they blaspheme that worthy name by the which ye are called?

8 If ye fulfil the royal law according to the scripture, Thou shalt love thy neighbour as thyself, ye do well.

1. Rich and poor (vv. 2-4).—The rich man obviously made his gold ring very conspicuous. He wanted people to know he was wealthy and expected special attention, which he got. But this was at the expense of a poor person, to whom it was made clear that his presence was not welcome. Does such discrimination exist in Christian congregations today? There is support in some quarters for the "homogeneous" congregation, comprised of one class of people. The fellowship is better, it is claimed. But can this be squared with Galatians 3:28? Or with what James said here?

2. Muddled thinking (vv. 5-7).—James gave two reasons this kind of discrimination was wrong. First, it ignored God's care for the poor. As the son of a village carpenter and a member of a large family, James had known what it meant to be poor. But God had come into his life to make him "rich in faith," a blessing he shared with many others. Second, it disregarded the fact that the church's persecutors were in the wealthy class.

3. Discrimination or courtesy (vv. 6-9).—Perhaps realizing that his previous statement might sound harsh, James hastened to say that if the reception given to a rich person was an act of courtesy, and not discrimination, that was in fulfillment of "the royal law" of love. But no individual should be given special treatment, for to do this was to transgress this royal law.

4. Words or works? (vv. 14:17).—How, then, should a Christian behave toward an obviously needy person? James said that kind words are not enough. They must be accompanied by kind deeds. Let the treatment of upper-crust individuals be balanced by appropriate behavior toward the underprivileged. For God in Christ loves us all.

APPLYING THE LESSON

The proof is in the action.—When Dick Williams, much-traveled baseball manager, was in Oakland he often had disputes with the umpires. He is sarcastic, and his sarcasm often came out in the arguments. On one occasion, he had a running argument with the home plate umpire all afternoon. Finally he said, "I am not going to complain about your calls on balls and strikes because if I do you will throw me out of the game." The umpire then asked him why he was out on the field if he wasn't going to complain. Dick Williams retorted, "I just wanted to tell you that you could go on 'What's My Line' wearing that chest protector and mask and carrying that indicator and no one on the panel would guess your occupation." What Dick Williams was saying was that the umpire's profession and his actions did not match.

James made the same complaint to the Christians of his day. If they refuse to confirm in their lives the claims they make with their lips, then those claims are of no value at all to the kingdom of God. Faith professed must be confirmed in daily life.

Perfectly filling the role.—A young lady had the lead part in a senior play during her college days. She worked hard on her part and after the performance was startled when a strange man came backstage and introduced himself to her as the author of the play. He said, "I just wanted to come back and tell you that I have seen this drama produced many times, but tonight you embodied what I envisioned for the heroine better than anyone else ever had. Tonight you made a dream of mine come true, you gave it flesh and blood, and I want to thank you."

The goal of every Christian should be to give flesh and blood to God's purpose for our lives, to be able to look in the mirror and see a true child of God.

The damage of the tongue.—Mark Twain used to say that it takes two people to injure us: an enemy to malign us and a friend to make sure we know what he said. Both culprits carry out their dastardly deed with the use of the tongue.

James repeatedly speaks of the power of the tongue, to bless or to curse, to build up or to tear down. The tongue is actually a barometer of our faith. That is, the control we exert over our tongue demonstrates the measure and maturity of our faith.

Each giving what he could.—Karen called Bonnie to see why she missed Sunday School the previous week. Bonnie explained that her father was in the hospital and her mother was going into the hospital to have another baby. Bonnie added, "I'm taking care of my three little brothers and could not get there."

When Karen reported to her Sunday School class the next week, all who were present were moved by Bonnie's predicament, and they all wanted to help. However, they were stymied because the need was so great.

After a moment of silence, one of the girls offered to help Bonnie clean the house. Another girl said, "I'll take some vegetables from our garden." Another offered, "My mother is a nurse. I know she will help them." Another one said, "I can sew. I'll make a gown for the baby." The teacher chimed in, "I'll ask my husband to go and cut their lawn." Someone else volunteered, "I'll go help her take care of the children." Others chimed in with suggestions of what they could do to help.

When the teacher reminded the class of the memory verse for the day, all of them got a kick out of it, for they had demonstrated the truth of the verse in their response to Bonnie's need. The verse was Acts 11:29 in *The Living Bible:* "So the believers decided to send relief to the Christians in Judea, each giving as much as he could."

What keeps us from responding to the "widows and orphans" of our day is not lack of resources but lack of compassion. When we really care, we will respond. And when we respond as these girls did, "each giving as much as he could," then we will be able to meet the needs of those who are around us. Compassion begins with the individual. But when it leads to group action, we discover that we can do together what we could not do alone.

TEACHING THE CLASS

Main Idea: Faith in Christ that results in salvation results in actions that are reflections of Him.

Suggested Teaching Aim: Learners will assess their own behavior and attitudes behind those actions to determine whether they reflect the way of Jesus Christ.

Introduce the Bible Study

Share the story "The proof is in the action" found in *Applying the Lesson*. Recall that this is the basic premise of James's writings. Ask: Why would James be so adamant that behavior is the statement of your faith? Elicit response. Establish that behavior grows out of what one believes. One's behavior accurately identifies the belief system. Words do not always accurately identify our beliefs.

A Teaching Outline

1. Consider the relationship of belief and behavior.
2. Discover James's teachings about the relationship of belief and behavior.
3. Evaluate personal behavior and attitudes as a measure of true belief in Christ.
4. Recommit hearts and behavior to Christ.

State that the purpose of this study is to help us to assess our own behaviors and our attitudes behind those behaviors to determine whether they reflect faith in Jesus Christ. Invite learners to turn in their Bibles to James 1.

Search for Biblical Truth

Display the following outline to guide the Bible searching.

BELIEF AND BEHAVIOR

1. Two Kinds of Listeners (Jas. 1:2-25)
   (1) Hearers only
   (2) Hearers who become doers
2. Two Kinds of Conduct (Jas. 1:26-27)
   (1) Uncontrolled; Self-deceived
   (2) Self-controlled; Self-denial
3. Two Kinds of People (Jas. 2:1-9,14-17)
   (1) The prejudiced and the unprejudiced
   (2) The sayers and the doers

Call attention to item 1 of the outline and the subheadings. Invite learners to read James 1:22-25 to themselves to discover James's description of these two types of listeners. Call for response. Share information about the reference to a glass, that is, a mirror, found in *Studying the Bible*. Ask rhetorically: Is it possible that when you come to listen on Sunday morning that you quickly glance in the mirror of what Christ wants you to be and soon forget? You therefore become a hearer only and not a hearer and doer of Jesus' teachings.

Note that verses 26-27 reflect two kinds of conduct. Call on a learner to read the verses aloud while others listen to learn what the two kinds of conduct are. Call for response. Ask: What does the man who does not bridle his tongue believe? What does the man who shows compassion and does not live like the world believe? Note that both men express their belief in their behavior. Share "The damage of the tongue" and "Each giving what he could" found in *Applying the Lesson*. Again remind learners that behavior is an accurate statement of what a person believes.

Call attention to item 3 on the outline and the subheadings. Call on a learner to read James 2:1-9 aloud. Call on another learner to read James 2:14-17 aloud. Ask: Why is giving special treatment to the rich person wrong? Is it always wrong? Elicit response. Use information from *Study the Bible* to draw conclusions.

Note that verses 14-17 are a succinct illustration of the difference in hearers and doers. Ask: Which tells more about what a person believes? (Neither tells more. Each is explicit.)

Give the Truth a Personal Focus

Ask rhetorically: If your behavior were observed, would you be in the category of people who "say" the right things but do nothing? What does that reveal about your faith and commitment to Jesus Christ? Invite learners to recommit their hearts and behavior to Jesus.

September 1990

Prophets, Priests, and Kings

Aids from BROADMAN for Studying and Teaching

Books:
An Introduction to the Old Testament and Its Study, Robert L. Cate
David: After God's Own Heart, H. Edwin Young
The Broadman Bible Commentary, Volumes 3,5,6
"Layman's Bible Book Commentary," Volumes 5,6,10,11,12,13

INTRODUCTION

We begin this new study year with a somewhat different approach to Old Testament history. We shall span the monarchy of Israel from inception to termination, fixing attention on significant events in that long story that brought about confrontation between rulers and God's messengers, the prophets.

Unit I will deal with the beginning of kingship under the title "Who Is Sovereign?" Samuel and Saul will first be seen in events that followed the people's demand for a king. Two lessons involving Nathan and David will follow, the prophet appearing as counselor and reprover.

September 2

Samuel and Saul

Basic Passages: 1 Samuel 8; 10:17-27

Focal Passage: 1 Samuel 10:17-25

History is written around outstanding personalities. Biblical history is no exception. From the first chapters of Genesis onward, events moved forward around leadership figures, men and women who either furthered or frustrated God's purposes. Not all of those who stood tall among their fellows proved themselves worthy of the responsibilities given to them. Saul is an outstanding example of this. As the first biblical character for our study in this new series of lessons, his story is told in relationship to another man, Samuel the prophet. The interaction between the two men sets the pattern for the quarter. A succession of kings will be considered in light of their response to the messages of prophets who, acting as God's representatives, offered either encouragement or rebuke. Human leadership must be evaluated and judged by divine standards. Some people may try to put themselves above the law but will eventually find themselves answerable to the laws of God.

Study Aim: *To consider the responsibilities both of those who choose leaders and of those who are chosen*

STUDYING THE BIBLE

This and the forthcoming studies are not intended to review the careers of selected Bible characters. They will serve to highlight incidents in which outstanding leaders were confronted by prophetic messengers who spoke in the name of God. Hence, each lesson will have a double focus. We shall study the leadership performance of some Old Testament kings and the function of prophets who were assigned by God to correct or affirm the conduct of these kings. As in the present case, we may need to go beyond the selected Bible passages to give substance to the lessons.

I. Demand for a King (1 Sam. 8)

This eighth chapter is included in the background material and is important to provide needed understanding of the circumstances in which Saul was chosen as Israel's first king.

1. Three reasons (vv. 5-20).—Samuel occupied a unique place in the history of Israel. He served as prophet, priest, and judge. Unfortunately, like Eli before him (2:12), his sons did not possess the integrity of their father. This supplied the first reason for the request for a king. The people rejected Samuel's sons as leaders. Two other reasons are found in verse 20. The Israelitish tribes were surrounded by nations that had kings. They wanted to get in step with their neighbors. In addition, they were threatened by some of these neighbors, particularly the Philistines, and desired kingship as a uniting force that would bring victory in battle.

2. The Lord consulted (vv. 6-9).—Samuel took this request as a personal affront. He was consistently a man of prayer (12:23), and he took his burden to God. He was told by God, "They have not rejected thee, but they have rejected me." The nation Israel had been established as a theocracy, that is, a people ruled by God. He had cared for them since the day He brought them out of Egypt. Nevertheless, Samuel was told he should accede to their wish. God does not coerce people into serving Him, but gives them the right of choice. Israel would live to regret the decision to embrace kingship (vv. 10-18). But God would overrule their mistake for good. The continuing Bible story tells how God selected a royal house, that of David, to provide the Messiah, who would be the Savior, not of Israel alone, but of all people.

II. Samuel Anoints Saul (1 Sam. 9:1–10:1)

One purpose of this lesson is to review the circumstances under which Israel's demand for a king was answered. God did not abdicate in light of this demand, but remained in control of events. The covenant between Him and His people was still in force. By it God had pledged Himself to seek Israel's highest welfare, and, through them, to bless the world. He used a human agent, Samuel, to identify the man who would be king, and involved the people as a whole in the process of his enthronement (10:17-27).

1. Lost donkeys (9:1-10).—The story of the lost asses must not blind us to the distinguished family background of Saul. His father, Kish, is described as "a mighty man of power," or, "wealth" (RSV). Saul himself had the physique for a king (v. 2). A person's wealth in those days was estimated in terms of his flocks and herds. The disappearances of the asses represented a considerable potential loss, and it is not surprising that the owner's son was sent to look for them.

2. Meeting with Samuel (vv. 15-21).—Saul's servant suggested that Samuel's help be sought in finding the lost animals (v. 6). God prepared Samuel in advance for the arrival of Saul by telling him, "Behold the man whom I spake to thee of! this same shall reign over my people" (v. 17). Samuel was engaged in priestly duties at the time and invited his visitor to join in the worship activities. Later he told Saul that the lost asses had been found and then astonished the young man by describing him as "the desire of Israel" (v. 20).

3. Anointing of Saul (9:25–10:1).—Graphic details attest to the truth of the record. After honoring Saul and his servant (v. 22) and providing them with comfortable lodging for the night, Samuel proceeded to take farewell of his two visitors. He accompanied them to "the outskirts of the city" (v. 27, RSV), at which point he told Saul to send his servant on ahead. Then, making clear that he was acting under instruction from God, the prophet anointed Saul's head with oil, a procedure previously followed in the appointment of priests and prophets. On his return home, Saul kept to himself what Samuel had said and done (10:15-16).

III. Saul Publicly Proclaimed (1 Sam. 10:17-27)

Now it was time for the presentation of the future king to his subjects. Samuel summoned a national assembly at Mizpeh, a significant location for the event. Mizpeh, or Mizpah (RSV), was the name of several Palestinian sites; but the reference is to a city in the tribe of Benjamin, to which Saul belonged. The place had become notable as the scene of a recent victory over the Philistines, granted in answer to prayer (7:5-12).

17 And Samuel called the people together unto the Lord to Mizpeh;

18 And said unto the children of Israel, Thus saith the Lord God of Israel, I brought up Israel out of Egypt, and delivered you out of the hand of the Egyptians, and out of the hand of all kingdoms, and of them that oppressed you;

19 And ye have this day rejected your God, who himself saved you out of all your adversities and your tribulations; and ye have said unto him, Nay, but set a king over us. Now therefore present yourselves before the Lord by your tribes, and by your thousands.

20 And when Samuel had caused all the tribes of Israel to come near, the tribe of Benjamin was taken.

21 When he had caused the tribe of Benjamin to come near by their families, the family of Matri was taken, and Saul the son of Kish was taken: and when they sought him, he could not be found.

22 Therefore they inquired of the Lord further, if the man

should yet come thither. And the Lord answered, Behold, he hath hid himself among the stuff.

23 And they ran and fetched him thence: and when he stood among the people, he was higher than any of the people from his shoulders and upward.

24 And Samuel said to all the people. See ye him whom the Lord hath chosen, that there is none like him among all the people? And all the people shouted, and said, God save the king.

25 Then Samuel told the people the manner of the kingdom, and wrote it in a book, and laid it up before the Lord. And Samuel sent all the people away, every man to his house.

1. Tribes assembled (vv. 17-19).—As yet, the Israelites were divided into twelve tribes that operated independently. In certain emergencies they cooperated against common enemies, but there was no central authority. By choosing Mizpeh for the assembly, a location equally accessible for the northern tribes as for the southern, Samuel facilitated their coming together. All were obligated to God for His deliverances, and all had shown ingratitude by their request for an earthly ruler instead of continuing to acknowledge God as sovereign Lord. The time would come when they would realize their mistake in such statements as, "It is better to trust in the Lord than to put confidence in princes" (Ps. 118:9).

2. Selction by elimination (vv. 20-23).—The method used in this public selection of a king is not clearly described. One translation reads, "The tribe of Benjamin was taken by lot" (v. 20, RSV). Apparently some type of ballot was employed so that, by a process of elimintation, the choice fell on Saul. Beginning with tribes, from which Benjamin was selected, and then casting lots family by family, the area of choice was narrowed to a single family, and the eventual nomination was Saul. But that young man was nowhere to be found. We must remember that he had been informed that he was God's choice, and it was not unnatural that he would shrink from the responsibility of national leadership. He had already shown a spirit of humility (9:21), and it is to his discredit that he allowed kingship to rob him of this laudable quality and replace it with pride and arrogance. Saul was found hiding in "the baggage" (v. 22, RSV), the traveling equipment used by the tribes on the respective journeys.

3. Conflicting reactions (vv. 24-27).—Not surprisingly, the people's choice (which was also God's) led to discontent and disagreement. The royalists were delighted that they had their ambitions fulfilled, and greeted Saul with the traditional salute:

"God save the king." Samuel, who had presided over this historic event, wrote "the manner of the kingdom" in a book. This document perhaps laid down the obligations and limitations of the monarchy, and the corresponding responsibilities of the people. Thus the proceedings were brought to a dignified conclusion. But there was a political opposition, as might be expected (v. 27), an early sign that Israel's monarchy would not be free from trouble. There are always those who will rebel against any form of authority and control.

4. Sad sequel (15:17-23).—Since our next lesson will introduce David as Saul's successor, it is not inappropriate that we make brief reference to the things that brought about Saul's downfall. He would allow himself to be consumed with jealousy against the youthful David. But, before this, he came under the judgment of God for an act of flagrant disobedience, described in 15:1-15. Not only did he transgress God's command, but also attempted to put the blame on others (v. 15). He was confronted by Samuel in a classic example of the way God's prophets were used to reprove kings for misconduct. This confrontation produced two memorable questions by Samuel. "When thou wast little in thine own sight, wast thou not made the head of the tribes of Israel, and the Lord anointed thee king over Israel?" (v. 17) was a reminder of the kind of person God can use for responsible tasks. "Hath the Lord as great delight in burnt offerings and sacrifices, as in obeying the voice of the Lord?" (v. 22) affirmed the unacceptability of religious activities that are not accompanied by obedient behavior.

APPLYING THE LESSON

By what standard?—Harriet Beecher Stowe was one of the most successful writers in American history. She achieved her first triumph as an author at the age of twelve. All students at Litchfield Academy were required to submit essays at the end of the term. Two of these papers were selected to be read at the graduation exercises by the headmaster, John Brace. The first prize was awarded to one of the papers by the unanimous vote of the judges. So outstanding was this paper, the audience applauded when it was read.

At that point it was revealed that Harriet Beecher, whose father Lyman was the pastor of the local church, was the author of this paper. The smile of her proud father was a reward she cherished as long as she lived. Her biographer said, "Neither the honors nor the success she won in later life meant as much to her, and, in effect, her career was determined."[1]

The approval of someone we admire makes a strong impact on our lives. However, each of us will eventually be judged by a higher standard. We see this tension between human approval and divine approval in the life of Israel's first king, Saul.

The power of fear.—According to Wayne Oates, the main fears we struggle with are the fear of abandonment by those we love, the fear of separation from the people we love or the job in which we find security, the fear of change, the fear of the condemnation of our own conscience, and the fear of losing control and becoming helpess. Perhaps, underlying all of these fears is the fear of death.

Fear can be a positive force, compelling us to accomplish things we would have otherwise left undone. Fear can also be a paralyzing force, preventing us from facing the challenges that need to be handled.

We see the power of fear to compel as it motivated the Israelites to ask for a king. We also see the power of fear to paralyze as Saul hid in the baggage as he was being elected king of Israel.

Prayer for guidance.—The pilot was obviously in trouble as he cried out for help. He finally was able to make radio contact with the tower: "Pilot to tower," he said, "I am 300 miles from land. I am only about 600 feet off the ground. I'm about out of gas. Please instruct." The man in the tower responded, "Tower to pilot. Repeat after me. 'Our Father, who art in heaven. . . .'"

Prayer is more than an emergency call to God when we need help. It is an opportunity to get in touch with God to make sure we do what is pleasing to Him. Samuel's prayer for guidance enabled him to provide proper direction for Israel in the selection of a new king.

God's ways are not our ways.—Martin Niemoeller who led in the opposition to Hitler in World War II, fought for the Germans in World War I. He was stationed on a German U-boat which almost sank a French ship off the coast of Dakar. Years later, Albert Schweitzer asked Niemoeller if he was on that German boat which tried to sink the French ship. Niemoeller replied that he was. Schweitzer explained that he was on that French ship and he was thankful that God spared him so that later, the two, Schweitzer and Niemoeller, could be comrades in the fight for peace.[2]

Sometimes God guides in ways we don't even understand at the time. This was the case with Saul. He thought he was simply trying to recover his lost donkeys. Instead, God was bringing him to a meeting with Samuel which would eventually lead to Saul's being crowned king of Israel.

True humility.—A preacher was leading a group of other preachers in a conference. Discussing various appropriate topics for a sermon, the leader said, "I have a magnificent sermon on humility, but I've not yet had a crowd big enough to preach it to!"

Much of what we present as "humility" is not real humility. Sometimes it is disguised pride as in the man who said, "At humility, we are tops!" At other times, it is nothing more than self-deprecation as in the little chorus we used to sing: "Nobody likes me, everybody hates me, I'm going to eat some worms!" Real humility is a rare quality, but it was evident in the life of Saul as he was elected Israel's first king.

TEACHING THE CLASS

Main Idea: Getting your own way may not be getting the way that is best for you.

Suggested Teaching Aim: Learners will evaluate the phenomenon of having it their own way.

Introduce the Bible Study

Introduce the three units that make up the study for this quarter. Note that the Scripture texts will be from the history of Israel. Remind learners that the purpose of the study will be to identify principles for guiding our own lives.

Write the title of unit I on the chalkboard. State that it is a question for which we know the correct answer but shaping our behaviors to reflect that answer is difficult. Note that wanting to have our own way is one of the reasons that shaping our behavior is difficult. Remind learners of the hamburger promotion that lets us know we can have it our own way. Note its appeal for all of us.

Continue by asking: Is it always a good thing to get your own way? Why or why not? What experience can you recall when getting your own way was a good thing? What experience can you recall that taught you that getting your own way is not always a good idea?

A Teaching Outline

1. Focus on having your own way.
2. Discover the details of a time when Israel insisted on having their own way.
3. Identify principles that apply to our effort to have our own way.

State that the study for today points up a time when Israel insisted on getting their own way. Note that our purpose is to learn from their experience some important principles about having our own way. Invite learners to open their Bibles to 1 Samuel 10:17-25.

Search for Biblical Truth

Share background information from *Studying the Bible*. Note three reasons given for Israel's strong desire to have a king. Share the comments from "The power of fear" *(Applying the Lesson).*

Briefly describe the anointing of Saul found in 1 Samuel 9:1—10:1. Note that the passage for study today picks up with the public presentation to the future king to Israel.

Call on a learner to read 1 Samuel 10:17-25 aloud while other learners listen to learn how Saul was publicaly chosen, why God agreed to provide a king, and the response of the people to the selection of the king. When the reading is finished, call for response. Share information from *Studying the Bible*.

Ask questions like the following to direct learners' thinking. Why was God reluctant to provide a king for Israel? What was the ultimate result of Israel's following a king? Was having their own way the best way for Israel? Why or why not?

Direct learners to spend some time working with those sitting near them to identify some principles related to wanting and getting our own way that grow out of this passage of Scripture. After several minutes, call for response.

The following principles may be used to supplement suggestions made by learners.

Principle 1: Getting your own way may cause you to forget what you have learned from the past. Note Samuel's effort to remind Israel in verses 17-18.

Principle 2: Getting your own way can cause you to reject those things most important to you. Note verse 19.

Principle 3: Getting your own way may impose on others. Note that Saul did not wish to be king.

Principle 4: Getting your own way may distort your vision. Note that Israel focused on Saul and not on God.

Principle 5: Getting your own way can be accompanied by the unexpected. Note verse 25. Samuel defined rules of the kingdom.

Give the Truth a Personal Focus

Close the study with illustration and comment from "God's ways are not our ways" from *Applying the Lesson*.

---

1. Noel B. Gerson, *Harriett Beecher Stowe* (New York: Praeger Publishers, Inc., 1976), 10.
2. Clarissa Stuart Davidson, *God's Man* (New York: Ives Washburn, 1959), 17.

September 9

Nathan and David

Basic Passage: 2 Samuel 7

Focal Passage: 2 Samuel 7:4-16

This is a chapter about two houses. David wanted to build a house (Temple) for the worship of God. This project was postponed as God promised to build a house (dynasty) for David. The play on the two meanings of the one word is an essential part of a record of relationship between Israel's king and God's prophet, Nathan. This man was a close friend of David's who named one of his sons Nathan (2 Sam. 5:14). The prophet was obviously disposed to support the king in projects he suggested. This was a sign of his friendship. But when God revealed to Nathan that he had been too hasty in giving his support, he did not hesitate to return to David and correct his mistake. Nathan was no less a friend when he said no than when he said yes. National leaders need advisers who will be impartially honest. So do we all. It is important that we learn that friendship need not always put us in the cheering section, but may sometimes influence us to criticize and condemn. Character is displayed when persons are willing to accept negative counsel from those who usually are positive in their response.

Study Aim: *To persuade us to submit our plans, however laudable they may appear, to the judgment of God*

STUDYING THE BIBLE

One of the reasons for Israel's request for a king was to unify the tribes into a fighting force that could subdue their enemies. To a large extent, this purpose was realized. Chapter 7 begins with reference to a time of peace that followed the repeated defeat of the Philistines recorded in 5:17-25.

I. A Commendable Project (2 Sam. 7:1-3)

The conquest of the land under Joshua left pockets of Canaanite resistance, notably "the strong hold of Zion" (5:7) that the Jebusites possessed. On its capture by David and his men, this fortress became known as "the city of David," or, Jerusalem. There, with the assistance of Hiram king of Tyre, David built himself a house (v. 11). He also caused the ark of the covenant to be brought into the city from "the house of Abinadab" (6:3) where it had been given temporary shelter after its recovery from the Philistines (1 Sam. 6:21; 7:1). A tent, or "tabernacle" was provided to shelter it (2 Sam. 6:17). The contrast between the splendor of his own home, and the simple accommodation provided for the ark, troubled David. This sacred object, that symbolized the presence of God among His people, surely merited a worthy building to house it. A plan to construct such a building was confided to Nathan who readily endorsed it.

II. God's Prophet Corrected (2 Sam. 7:4-7)

No doctrine of infallibility is expounded in Scripture for priest or prophet. They were mortal men, capable of making mistakes, except when they spoke as mouthpieces for God. Their "thus saith the Lord" was the seal of inspiration on their utterances. In 1 Chronicles 29:29, Nathan is named as a chronicler of events in the life of David. It is reasonable to suppose, therefore, that he was responsible for preserving the records of his own mistaken judgment.

> **4 And it came to pass that night, that the word of the Lord came unto Nathan, saying,**
>
> **5 Go and tell my servant David, Thus saith the Lord, Shalt thou build me a house for me to dwell in?**
>
> **6 Whereas I have not dwelt in any house since the time that I brought up the children of Israel out of Egypt, even to this day, but have walked in a tent and in a tabernacle.**
>
> **7 In all the places wherein I have walked with all the children of Israel spake I a word with any of the tribes of Israel, whom I commanded to feed my people Israel, saying, Why build ye not me an house of cedar?**

Another argument against David's plan to build a temple is given in 1 Chronicles 28:3, "But God said unto me, Thou shalt not build an house for my name, because thou hast been a man of war, and hast shed blood." This passage goes on to say, "Solomon thy son, he shall build my house" (v. 6). Our study verses, therefore, should not be interpreted as a prohibition against the provision of a central sanctuary, but as a postponement. God seemed to be saying to David, through Nathan, "Don't be in too much hurry. All these years the ark of My presence has been housed in a tent. It traveled with the people, a constant reminder that I was in their midst. Not once have I expressed a preference for any other kind of accommodation. Don't run ahead of me, David." The time would come when Jerusalem's Temple would become an object of superstitious trust (Jer. 7:4). There was, and is, need for a constant reminder that God's presence is not secured by any type of construction, but that "the most High dwelleth not in temples made with hands" (Acts 7:48).

III. A Message for David (2 Sam. 7:8-11)

One of the earliest recorded acts of rebellion against God is introduced by the words, "Go to, let us build" (Gen. 11:4). People have often been inclined to memorialize themselves by erecting impressive buildings. The much-admired cathedrals of Europe were, in some cases, expressions of human pride more than salutes to the greatness of God. Cities and their rulers sought to outdo their neighbors by the splendor of their church architecture. This fault is not absent from Christian circles today. While there is no direct statement in our study chapter that David had anything other than the purest motive in proposing to build a sanctuary for God, the verses which follow indicate that the Lord saw need for reminding this king of his humble origins. Success in life invariably brings the temptation to claim personal credit for achieving it. The best of persons succumb to this temptation with corresponding adverse effects on character and disposition. God cared too much for David, a man "after his own heart" (1 Sam. 13:14; Acts 13:22), to allow him to slip into this mold. Credit must be given to God alone for David's progress from shepherd to king ("I took thee from the sheepcote," v. 8), and for his victories over Israel's enemies ("I was with thee . . . and have cut off all thine enemies," v. 9).

8 Now therefore so shalt thou say unto my servant David, Thus saith the Lord of hosts, I took thee from the sheepcote, from following the sheep, to be ruler over my people, over Israel:

9 And I was thee whithersoever thou wentest, and have cut off all of thine enemies out of thy sight, and have made thee a great name, like unto the name of the great men that are in the earth.

10 Moreover I will appoint a place for my people Israel and will plant them, that they may dwell in a place of their own, and move no more; neither shall the children of wickedness afflict them anymore, as beforetime.

11 And as since the time that I commanded judges to be over my people Israel, and have caused thee to rest from all thine enemies. Also the Lord telleth thee that he will make thee an house.

David was a warrior-king who yet had many battles to fight before his kingdom was secure. The capture of Zion from the Jebusites and the repeated defeat of the Philistines did not remove every threat to the newly established kingdom. The continuing narrative tells how he fought against the Moabites, Syrians, and Edomites (8:1-13), and later the Ammonites (chap. 10). David, therefore, was premature in proposing to celebrate peace by the erection of the Temple. God's plans for His people were strong and firm. "I will appoint a place for my people Israel, and will plant them, that they may dwell in a place of their own and move no more" (v. 10). But this was in the future, and David's task was to lead the now united nation into victory over all its enemies. When that time came, and his throne was firmly established, a new divine promise would come into effect, "the Lord telleth thee that he will make thee an house" (v. 11). The significance of this promise must be explored in the following verses.

IV. A Throne and a Kingdom (2 Sam. 7:12-17)

The man who was forbidden to build a house (Temple) for God was promised a house (dynasty) by God. The line of kings that descended from David became known as "the house of David" (Isa. 7:2, 13). After David came Solomon, to whom specific promises were given in the following verses. He would be permitted to build a Temple to God in Jerusalem (v. 13), a task that he carried out as recorded in 1 Kings 6—7, a passage that concludes, "So was ended all the work that king Solomon made for the house of the Lord" (7:51). This splendid edifice became known as Solomon's Temple and lasted until the Babylonian destruction of Jerusalem in 587 B.C. For him was repeated the promise given to David, "I will stablish the throne of his kingdom for ever" (v. 13). The Lord would not coddle him. When David sinned, he would be punished (v. 14). But God would not abandon him, as He had earlier withdrawn His favor from Saul (v. 15). Through Solomon and his descendants would be fulfilled the promise previously given to David, and now repeated, "Thy throne shall be established for ever" (v. 16). Following Solomon's death, the kingdom would be divided, ten of the tribes seceding in order to form the Northern Kingdom of Israel. The house of David continued to rule over Jerusalem and Judea and outlasted the Northern Kingdom by some 135 years. Did the Babylonian captivity mean that the promise of an everlasting kingdom failed?

12 And when thy days be fulfilled, and thou shalt sleep with thy

fathers, I will set up thy seed after thee, which shall proceed out of thy bowels, and I will establish his kingdom.

13 He shall build an house for my name, and I will stablish the throne of his kingdom forever.

14 I will be his father, and he shall be my son. If he commit iniquity, I will chasten him with a rod of men, and with the stripes of the children of men:

15 But my mercy shall not depart away from him, as I took it from Saul, whom I put away before thee.

16 And thine house and thy kingdom shall be established forever before thee: thy throne shall be established forever.

The words we are studying were spoken by Nathan, who was given them by God (v. 4). As the Lord's prophet, he spoke to the immediate circumstances, David's desire to build a temple for the worship of God. But, whether Nathan realized this or not, his prophecy of the future reached far beyond the occupants of David's throne to a time when "great David's greater son," the Lord Jesus Christ, would claim for Himself the throne of the universe over which He would reign throughout eternity. On the stage of human history it might appear as though the Davidic line of kings came to an end with Zedekiah (2 Kings 25:1-7). But the purposes of God embraced a kingdom greater than Israel at the peak of its prosperity. The New Testament is introduced as, "The book of the generation of Jesus Christ, the Son of David" (Matt. 1:1), and the angel's announcement to Mary was in these terms, "And behold, thou shalt conceive in thy womb, and bring forth a son, and shalt call his name Jesus. He shall be great, and shall be called the Son of the Highest: and the Lord God shall give unto him the throne of his father David: And he shall reign over the house of Jacob forever; and of his kingdom there shall be no end" (Luke 1:31-33). Nathan's prophecy was messianic. It has had part fulfillment in the birth and ministry of the Lord Jesus. It awaits complete fulfillment in that day when, "The kingdom of the world has become the kingdom of our Lord and of his Christ, and he shall reign for ever and ever" (Rev. 11:15, RSV).

APPLYING THE LESSON

I'd better listen to him.—At a period of crisis in the Civil War, Lincoln sent some instructions to Stanton his Secretary of War. The messenger returned in obvious embarrassment. "Did you deliver the message?" the President inquired. "Yes, sir," the young man responded. "And what did he say?" After a few seconds of hesitation, the young man answered, "Mr. Stanton tore up your letter and he called you a fool." There was a moment of silence. Finally, Lincoln replied, "Mr. Stanton is generally right. I had better look into the matter."

With some criticism you merely consider the source and ignore it. Criticism from certain sources, however, demands attention. When the prophet Nathan revealed his criticism of David, David listened.

God's timing.—One of the greatest sins among Christians today is the sin of impatience. Charles Allen, famous Methodist minister, calls it the sin of staying too busy. Noah waited nearly 100 years after he built the ark for God's judgment to come. Moses waited in the wilderness 40 years as God prepared him for his mission. Abraham and Sarah had to wait until they were almost 100 for God to fulfill His promise of a son. In contrast, we have a nervous breakdown waiting for a revolving door to come around!

William Carey began the modern missionary movement in his pioneering work for Christ in India. Before he was through he had translated the Bible into 36 different languages. He planted churches and won converts and established medical work all over that part of the world. What we often forget is that Carey went to India in 1793. And he won his first convert in 1800, seven years after he arrived! Carey faithfully and patiently carried out his work for God, even without the visible results, because he knew God's timing was not his timing.

This is a lesson David had to learn. He desired to build a house for God, but it had to be in God's timing and according to God's plan.

Two for one.—A little boy came up to President Hoover just after he had left the White House and asked him for his autograph. After the President had graciously complied, the little boy said, "Would you mind signing your name again a little further down on the paper?" Again the President obliged, but his curiosity prompted him to ask, "Why twice?" The boy explained, "Because, with two of yours I can get one of Babe Ruth's."

As great as a person thinks he is, he is probably not as great as he thinks he is! Pride is a constant enemy every person has to confront. David knew of this struggle. He had accomplished much in his lifetime. He had to constantly struggle against the temptation to say, "Look what I have done" instead of saying, "Look what God has done through me."

Starting and finishing.—Someone once asked Henry Ford the secret of his success. He said, "When you start a thing, finish it."

That's good advice. Good beginnings do not necessarily ensure good endings. Many have gone up like a flash and then quickly come down like a fluke. The secret of accomplishment for God is to finish what we start, to complete the assignments God gives to us. God wanted David to establish Israel in the land by defeating all the enemies. To accomplish this, David had to persist at the task.

The Hallelujah Chorus.—At the death of Dr. F. B. Meyer, noted preacher and teacher, he had already made the plans for his funeral service. At the heart of the service, which Meyer developed himself, was the singing of the Hallelujah Chorus. How can we sing the Hallelujah Chorus at the time of death? Because we know that death is not a defeat but a victory. It is not the end but simply a new beginning.

The plan of God is not dependent upon any one individual. Even when David was gone, the work of God would continue.

TEACHING THE CLASS

Main Idea: Even a good thing may not be the right thing.

Suggested Teaching Aim: Learners will commit themselves to seeking the mind of God, even in things that are inherently good.

Introduce the Bible Study

Ask: Did you ever see a good thing turn out bad? Pause a moment for learners to think of such an experience. Continue: What is it that can cause a good thing to turn out bad? Elicit response.

State that the study for today explores David's experience with something that was inherently good but that was not approved by God. Note that it will show us more about why it is difficult for us to keep God sovereign in our lives. Invite learners to open their Bibles to 2 Samuel 7:4-16.

Search for Biblical Truth

Invite learners to scan verses 1-3 to discover what good thing David wanted to do. Elicit response. Continue by asking: Why did David want to build a house for God? What was Nathan's response to David's idea? Who was Nathan?

A Teaching Outline

1. Identify something inherently good that turned out bad.
2. Explore the experience of David when something inherently good was not approved by God.
3. Identify reasons that David's good idea was not approved by God.
4. Commit themselves to seeking the mind of God even about their own ideas that are inherently good.

Invite a learner to read verses 4-7 aloud while other learners listen to discover an unexpected event that followed. When the reading is finished, call for response.

Note that the message Nathan was to deliver goes on in verses 8-11. Call on a learner to read the message aloud. When the reading is finished, ask questions like the following. What was God's reminder to David? What was the task that God wanted to accomplish through David?

Note that while God did not approve David's good idea, He did give David a glimpse into the future. This allowed David to know that a house for God was a good idea. Call on a learner to read verses 12-16 aloud. When the reading is finished, ask: What was the glimpse into the future provided by God? How was that an encouragement to David?

Share the story titled "I'd better listen to him" found in *Applying the Lesson*. Ask: Why would King David be willing to listen to Nathan?

Direct learners to work with those sitting near them to identify reasons that David's good idea was not approved by God. Allow several minutes for discussion. Call for conclusions.

Responses should include the following, supplement learners' responses as necessary.

1. God's priority was not David's priority. Note that God's work for David was to establish Israel in the land so that they would be protected from their enemies. Share the story titled "Starting and finishing" *(Applying the Lesson).*

2. Timing makes a lot of difference in the effect that a good thing produces. Note that David's idea was approved by God but for a later date. Share the story titled "God's timing" *(Applying the Lesson).*

3. Credit for a good thing frequently should be shared. Note that Solomon, David's son, would share the credit for the Temple. Share the story "Two for one" in *Applying the Lesson*.

Give the Truth a Personal Focus

Review the reasons that the good thing which David had in mind was not the right thing. Invite learners to recall the good thing that turned out bad for them mentioned as the lesson was begun. Ask: Is it possible that one of these reasons is the explanation for your good idea coming out bad? Continue: How can you know whether the good idea you have is the right idea or not? Elicit response that indicates that seeking the mind of God is necessary even in choices that involve good things.

Invite learners to commit themselves to seeking the mind of God in implementing good things in their lives.

September 16

Nathan Rebukes David

Basic Passage: 2 Samuel 11:1—12:25

Focal Passages: 2 Samuel 12:1-10,13

The basic honesty of the biblical narrative, concerning its leading characters, is one of its appealing features. Its heroes wear no haloes. The achievements and successes, even their attainment of spiritual goals, are recorded against a background of human frailty. They were not supermen and superwomen, but mortals such as ourselves, capable of gaining great heights, but at the same time susceptible to Satan's wiles. If at times they rose above the level of average persons, this was because they trusted more in God than in themselves. When they failed to do this, they left themselves open to temptations and had no power to resist. David is an outstanding example of this, while Nathan provides an example of that prophetic mission that must reprove sin even when found in persons of highest rank and closest friendship. We might ask ourselves if prophetic voices are needed today to challenge sin whether indulged in by individuals or nations. Have we such prophetic voices?

Study Aim: *To affirm that sin is sin, and is so regarded by the Lord, regardless of the social position of the offender*

STUDYING THE BIBLE

Our basic passage provides comprehensive coverage of the reasons why God's prophet was sent to reprove the conduct of a divinely appointed king. We shall need to use the greater part of the two chapters to provide an adequate outline for this lesson.

I. David's Double Transgression (2 Sam. 11:1-17)

The Bible offers no excuse for David's conduct. We may claim that the things he did, first adultery and then murder, were normal behavior for Oriental monarchs. But David was not a run-of-the-mill king. He was God's chosen ruler for His Chosen People and, therefore, bound to a higher standard of conduct than his pagan counterparts.

1. Bathsheba (vv. 1-5).—From the flat roof of his palace, Israel's king saw a neighbor's wife, coveted her, took her, and committed adultery with her. The setting was typical of the time and place, and the circumstances common to every culture, country, and race. Adultery is a universal sin, and it sometimes entraps the most unlikely people. Sexual desire can only be controlled by rigid self-discipline aided by the grace of God. Unhappily, adultery is treated lightly in many quarters today. But Exodus 20:14 states the biblical standard.

2. Uriah (vv. 6-17).—One sin led to another. David tried to cover his sin by bringing Bathsheba's husband home from the battle front, supposing that he would sleep with his wife. But in commitment to his military code, Uriah refused to do this. So David took the extreme course of having this exemplary man exposed to danger on the battlefield. He was killed by an Ammonite arrow, and, in unseemly haste, David brought Bathsheba into the palace. Too many people seek to achieve selfish ends by violence.

II. Nathan's Parable (2 Sam. 12:1-6)

Nathan's role was both difficult and dangerous. Time had passed since the king's dual offense, time enough for the child of the adulterous union to be born (11:27). Psalm 32:3-4 encourages the belief that David's conscience had been troubling him. But nobody had stood forward to rebuke him until the Lord charged Nathan with that task.

1 And the Lord sent Nathan unto David. And he came unto him, and said unto him, There were two men in one city; the one rich, and the other poor.

2 The rich man had exceeding many flocks and herds:

3 But the poor man had nothing, save one little ewe lamb, which he had bought and nourished up: and it grew up together with him, and with his children; it did eat of his own meat, and drank of his own cup, and lay in his bosom, and was unto him as a daughter.

4 And there came a traveler unto the rich man, and he spared to take of his own flock and of his own herd, to dress for the wayfaring man that was come unto him; but took the poor man's lamb, and dressed it for the man that was come to him.

5 And David's anger was greatly kindled against the man; and he said to Nathan, As the Lord liveth, the man that hath done this thing shall surely die:

6 And he shall restore the lamb fourfold, because he did this thing, and because he had no pity.

1. The story (vv. 1-4).—The prophet showed wisdom by taking an indirect approach to a delicate subject. He told of an incident that may have been an invention of his mind, or, on the other hand, an actual happening with which he had become acquainted. A man bought a lamb and made it a family pet. It gave great pleasure to him and his children. In their poverty they experienced few of the good things of life that were enjoyed daily by their wealthy neighbor. One day, this neighbor had a surprise visitor. To furnish a meal for his guest, he took and killed the ewe lamb, passing over the animals in his own extensive flocks. (The phrase "ewe lamb" has passed into common usage to describe a unique family treasure.)

2. Royal reaction (vv. 5-6).—David's wrath was stirred by the callous conduct reported to him. As king, cases were brought before him for judgment, and, in this case, he was quick to say that the offender deserved to die. However, he showed one of the better aspects of his nature by rejecting the supreme penalty in favor of a principle of Hebrew law already established (Ex. 22:1). The poor man must be paid four times the value of the lamb to compensate for his loss.

III. A King Indicted (2 Sam. 12:7-12)

In one of the most dramatic moments of biblical history, Nathan pointed an accusing finger at David, and said, "Thou art the man." This must have been a painful moment for the prophet who had been charged by God (v. 1) to make plain to the occupant of Israel's throne that he was as responsible before the Lord for his sins as any of his subjects. Unfortunately, the idea that "the king can do no wrong" was acceptable in many cultures, and has persisted in similar form down the centuries. He who is no respecter of persons holds all equally accountable and equally subject to His judgments.

7 And Nathan said to David, Thou art the man. Thus saith the Lord God of Israel, I anointed thee king over Israel, and I delivered thee out of the hand of Saul;

8 And I gave thee thy master's house, and thy master's wives into thy bosom, and gave thee the house of Israel and of Judah; and if that had been too little, I would moreover have given unto thee such and such things.

9 Wherefore hast thou despised the commandment of the Lord, to do evil in his sight? thou hast killed Uriah the Hittite with the sword, and hast taken his wife to be thy wife, and hast slain him with the sword of the children of Ammon.

10 Now therefore the sword shall never depart from thine house; because thou hast despised me, and hast taken the wife of Uriah the Hittite to be thy wife.

1. Sins exposed (vv. 7-9).—Following prevailing custom, David had taken possession of all his predecessor Saul's property, including his wives. Nathan's frank acknowledgment of existing polygamy is shocking to us, as indeed it should be. God permitted this practice for a period, but He did not approve of it. The Scriptures abound in evidence of the evils that flowed from this custom. They were revealed in David's family. This king, appointed by God to his office (v. 7), was doubly guilty in that he took another man's wife and arranged his death to cover his adultery.

2. Consequences stated (vv. 10-12).—This violation of another man's family rights, together with the taking of his life, was more than a social transgression. The sin was against God Himself, "Thou hast despised me" (v. 10). In a great psalm of confession, possibly related to this incident, David would say, "Against thee, thee only, have I sinned, and done this evil in thy sight" (Ps. 51:4). The commandments against murder and adultery were written plainly into the law (Ex. 20:13-14), and their breach must be the occasion for divine judgment. The continuing story tells of the sorrow that David experienced from treachery and intrigue, some of it within his own family.

IV. David's Repentance (2 Sam. 12:13-14)

We should not assume that the words of confession and repentance recorded in verse 13 cover all that was said in this encounter between king and prophet. Psalms 32 and 51, attributed by many to David, reveal the depth of his emotion as he faced up to the gravity of his sins.

13 And David said unto Nathan, I have sinned against the Lord. And Nathan said unto David, The Lord also hath put away thy sin; thou shalt not die.

1. Confession and forgiveness (v. 13).—Nathan's reply to David's confession, "The Lord also hath put away thy sin," is full of important theological implication. David's sin was not overlooked because he was king. Neither were its consequences avoided. Verses 10 and 11 summarize the tragic happenings that would cast deep shadows over David's remaining years. But because of the sincerity of David's repentance, God promised through His prophet to "put away" his sin. God would not ignore it, but deal with it redemptively and justly. Though the way God would do this was not yet revealed, we have the New Testament's teaching on the substitutionary nature of Christ's death "for every man" (Heb. 2:9). That basic gospel text, "God so loved the world" (John 3:16), does not limit that redeeming love to the New Testament period, but includes every age and every person. Forgiveness granted in Old Testament times anticipated the atoning work of the Lord Jesus who is the Savior of all who believe.

2. A child's death (v. 14).—Part of the tragedy of sin is the effect it has on others. David lived, but Bathsheba's child died. Thus the woman was also involved in the penalty for adultery. Again let it be said that divine forgiveness does not take away the horrible harvest of sin. A person who lives in reckless disregard of moral laws, and is converted, may carry the marks of a dissolute life to the grave. But his forgiveness is real and his salvation assured. The royal grief over the fatal sickness of Bathsheba's son is graphically recorded in verses 15-23.

3. Another son (vv. 24-25).—God's promises to David concerning the enduring qualities of his "house" remained firm. Though one child died, another was born. The father named him Solomon (Peaceable) and Nathan gave him the name Jedidiah (Beloved of God). Thus the succession was assured and the Davidic line continued, to lead eventually to the birth of Jesus proclaimed "King of kings, and Lord of lords" (Rev. 19:16).

APPLYING THE LESSON

My crowd.—A man who had been shopping around for a church home stopped in one church just in time to hear the pastor say, "We have left undone those things which we ought to have done, and we have done those things which we ought not to have done." The man dropped into a pew and sighed with relief: "I've found my crowd at last."

We all belong in that crowd, for even as Christians we are sinners still. Lest we point an accusative finger at David, we need to remember that we are sinners just as he was.

I want to know why.—The woman was sharing with her pastor about a recent discovery. Her husband was having an affair. In her anguish, the wife said to the pastor, "I want to know why."

The why of affairs is not easy to pinpoint. Sometimes infidelity is the result of curiosity or a desire for variety combined with opportunity. Or an affair stems from sexual problems within a marriage. Infidelity is often the result of an identity crisis of one of the partners, particularly in midlife. At the root of all infidelity is a misunderstanding of the seriousness of faithfulness, and a lack of personal discipline.

David's infidelity came as a result of an extended time of inactivity and a chance opportunity when he saw Bathsheba bathing.

The right approach.—Belford managed to get an interview with a tough, hard-to-sell sales manager. He walked into his office and said, "I don't suppose you want any life insurance do you?" "I certainly don't," shouted the sales manager. Belford, head bowed, started toward the door. "Wait a minute," said the manager. "It's my job to train salesmen at this plant and I want you to know you are the worst salesman I've ever seen. You need some help." For an hour, Belford listened to a lecture on salesmanship by this highly successful sales manager. By the time he had finished, the sales manager had worked himself up to such a pitch that he signed an order for a $250,000 insurance policy. He handed it to the salesman and said, "Remember, the first thing to do is to learn a couple of standard, organized approaches." Belford replied, "I've already done that. I have an approach for every type of prospect. What you've seen today was my standard approach to tough sales managers!"

This salesman realized that the success of his venture depended on his approach. Likewise, when Nathan approached David to confront him with his sin, he realized the importance of the right approach. He used an indirect approach and let David provide the conclusion.

Distorted morality.—A man came to the doctor with an ulcer. The doctor asked him if there was any undue stress that might be causing the problem. The married man admitted that he had a girlfriend in Syracuse and that he frequently drove an old pickup truck down to see her. The pickup would regularly break down so he had to devise many stories to tell his wife. The doctor told him that he had to make some hard decisions about his personal priorities if he was to ever get well.

The patient bumped into the doctor about six months later and informed him that he was completely cured. The doctor congratulated him and then delicately inquired if he'd made some change in his life. "Yes," admitted the man, "I bought a new pickup."

We often deal with our moral dilemmas in such a distorted way. We change everything except the one thing we need most to change.

Sowing and reaping.—There is a law of consequences in life which applies to every person. What we sow, we will reap. Most of us sow our wild oats and then go to church and pray for a crop failure. Robert Louis Stevenson was more realistic when he said, "Everybody soon or late sits down to a banquet of consequences." This law of life even applied to the great King David.

TEACHING THE CLASS

Main Idea: Sin entraps the sinner, results in damage, and has lasting consequences.

Suggested Teaching Aim: Learners will identify some guidelines for dealing with the entrapping effects of sin and commit themselves to vigilance.

Introduce the Bible Study

Share the story "My crowd" found in *Applying the Lesson*. Note that most of us can identify with the man. Sin easily entraps us.

Continue the discussion by asking: What are some subtle ways that sin can move into our lives and trap us? Are you always aware of the threat of sin? Are you always aware of the presence of sin in your life? How do you most frequently discover that you have been trapped? Elicit response.

State that the study for today is a familiar story about the entrapment of sin, the story of David and Bathsheba. Note that the purpose of the study is to identify some guidelines that we will use to deal with the threat of sin in our own lives.

Search for Biblical Truth

Write these four names on the chalkboard: David, Bathsheba, Uriah, Nathan. Invite learners to identify each of the persons. Supplement with information from *Studying the Bible* as necessary.

A Teaching Outline

1. Consider ways sin subtly traps us.
2. Discover David's experience when he was trapped by sin.
3. Identify some principles to deal with the entrapping effect of sin in our own lives.
4. Commit themselves to awareness and resistance of sin.

Share the story "I want to know why" found in *Applying the Lesson*. Note the circumstances in which sin laid a snare for King David.

Invite learners to open their Bibles to 2 Samuel 12:1-6. Share the story "The right approach" *(Applying the Lesson)*. State that Nathan's approach to David to confront him with his sin was a masterpiece. Call on a learner to read verses 1-6 aloud.

Note that now that David was dealing with this sin, Nathan under the direction of God, showed David that it was David himself who was trapped. Call on a learner to read verses 7-12 aloud. When the reading is finished, ask: What is the sin that has trapped David? (Note v. 10: "Thou hast despised me. . . .") What is the consequence of that sin? Elicit response.

Ask: How did David respond? Invite a learner to read aloud verse 13. Note that these are not to be considered all the words David spoke revealing the depth of his emotions about his sin.

Other words are recorded in Psalms 32 and 51. Call on two learners who have previously agreed to read these psalms aloud.

Display the following principles that can help us deal with the entrapment of sin in our lives. Direct learners to search the Scripture passage to identify verses that support each stated principle. Write the verses after each principle as learners suggest them.

Principle 1: Sin that is obvious in others is often hidden in ourselves. (vv. 1-7)

Principle 2: Sin is an affront to God's generosity to us. (vv. 7*b*-9*a*)

Principle 3: A single sin entraps and leads to other sins. (v. 9)

Principle 4: Sin has lasting consequences. (vv. 9-10)

Principle 5: God's grace is greater than the strength of sin in a life. (v. 13).

Share the story "Distorted morality" *(Applying the Lesson)* in the discussion of principle 1. Share "Sowing and reaping" when discussing principle 4.

Give the Truth a Personal Focus

Ask: In what way can we apply these principles to guard against the traps of sin in our own lives? Encourage learners to respond with things to do and ways to act as safeguards against the traps of sin. Conclude with a time of prayer inviting learners to commit themselves to awareness and resistance of sin.

September 23

Elijah and Ahab

Basic Passage: 1 Kings 21

Focal Passages: 1 Kings 21:4-11*a*,17-19

The tribes united under David became a divided kingdom after the death of Solomon. The heir to the throne, Rehoboam, acted unwisely when request was made for burdens imposed by Solomon to be lifted. As a consequence, ten of the tribes followed Jeroboam and declared themselves an independent state. Rehoboam remained king of Judah, with Jerusalem as his capital, while Jeroboam chose Samaria as his capital and established religious practices that led to idolatry (1 Kings 12). The two territories became known as Judah and Israel respectively. Our lesson deals with conditions in the Northern Kingdom, Israel, under the reign of Ahab, seventh ruler of that separated country. Of this man the statement is made that "there was none like unto Ahab, which did sell himself to work wickedness in the sight of the Lord" (1 Kings 21:25). During his reign, God spoke through Elijah the Tishbite (17:1), a man whose background is unknown beyond the contents of this verse. His name means "My God is Yahweh," significant enough for a prophet who stood against idolatry and for righteousness and justice.

Study Aim: *To recognize that corruption and injustice in government and individuals are evils that incur divine judgment*

STUDYING THE BIBLE

Ahab married a woman whose name has come to stand for everything evil. Jezebel was daughter to Ethbaal, king of Tyre, a pagan ruler who promoted debased forms of idolatry. Ahab yielded to the religious pressures of his wife and himself became a worshiper of Baal (1 Kings 16:30-33). This surrender to idolatry occasioned the initial appearance of Elijah (17:1) who persuaded Ahab to allow a confrontation between the priests of Baal and God's prophet at Carmel (18:19-40). He thereby incurred the murderous hatred of Jezebel, from whom he fled for his life (chap. 19). But when God called him to face the royal pair with a message of divine judgment, Elijah responded.

I. A Coveted Vineyard (1 Kings 21:1-4)

The occasion was a crime committed against a helpless man named Naboth. David saw a woman and coveted her for himself. Ahab saw a piece of neighboring property and determined to possess it. Both men transgressed the Tenth Commandment. "Thou shalt not covet," a commandment that specifically mentions "thy neighbor's wife . . . nor any thing that is thy neighbor's" (Ex. 20:17). Covetousness unrestrained inevitably leads to crime.

1. Naboth's refusal (v. 3).—Real estate was held in trust in Israel, ownership passing from generation to generation, so that it was family property and not the possession of an individual. Thus, though Ahab offered to pay Naboth for his vineyard, he was not free to sell it. To him it was "the inheritance of my fathers," his to enjoy only for the length of his life.

2. Ahab's reaction (v. 4).—Ahab knew the legalities of Naboth's refusal, but did not cease to covet his vineyard. Desire became an obsession. He was not used to being refused. Like a spoiled child, he sulked and lost his appetite.

> **4 And Ahab came into his house heavy and displeased because of the word which Naboth the Jezreelite had spoken to him: for he had said, I will not give thee the inheritance of my fathers. And he laid him down upon his bed, and turned away his face, and would eat no bread.**

II. A Dastardly Plot (1 Kings 21:5-14)

There must have been a smidgin of decency in Ahab that restrained him from taking what he wanted. This bewildered his wife, Jezebel. She believed in an absolute monarchy in which the ruler did whatever he chose, regardless. This reflected her parentage and upbringing. According to Edesheim,[1] her father was originally high priest of Astarte, the female consort to Baal. He murdered his king and usurped the throne. Jezebel was completely devoted to the sex-ridden religion of her father and, accordingly, had no respect for Israel's laws, which were the laws of Israel's God.

> **5 But Jezebel his wife came to him, and said unto him, Why is thy spirit so sad, that thou eatest no bread?**
>
> **6 And he said unto her, Because I spake unto Naboth the Jezreelite, and said unto him. Give me thy vineyard for money; or else, if it please thee, I will give thee another vineyard for it: and he answered, I will not give thee my vineyard.**
>
> **7 And Jezebel his wife said unto him, Dost thou now govern the kingdom of Israel? arise, and eat bread, and let thine heart be merry: I will give thee the vineyard of Naboth the Jezeelite.**
>
> **8 So she wrote letters in Ahab's name, and sealed them with his seal, and sent the letters unto the elders and to the nobles that were in his city, dwelling with Naboth.**
>
> **9 And she wrote in the letters, saying, Proclaim a fast, and set Naboth on high among the people:**
>
> **10 And set two men, sons of Belial, before him, to bear witness against him, saying, Thou didst blaspheme God and the king. And then carry him out, and stone him, that he may die.**
>
> **11 And the men of his city, even the elders and the nobles who were the inhabitants in his city, did as Jezebel had sent unto them.**

1. Partners in crime (vv. 5-8).—To Jezebel, Naboth's refusal may have appeared totally unreasonable, since Ahab had offered either money or an alternative piece of land. But her method for obtaining the vineyard was without excuse, and, in fact, criminal.

She comforted her peeved husband with smooth words, something she had probably done many times before, and then set in motion a diabolical plot to get rid of Naboth. It is not possible to believe that the letters were written, and sealed with the royal seal, without Ahab's knowledge. The seal was a symbol of his office and would have been kept in safety. Hence, Ahab was guilty of complicity, and was later charged by God with responsibility for the death of Naboth (v. 19).

2. The evil scheme (vv. 9-10).—The scene of this drama was Jezreel, a mountain town northeast of Samaria, where Ahab had his summer palace. It thus became a royal city, and, in this case, of an evil queen. Local property owners constituted a town council which normally would stand firmly for the rule of law. But in this case, royal patronage meant royal control. Letters bearing Ahab's seal had to be obeyed, whatever their demand. Consequently, Jezebel's cruel plan proceeded without question.

3. Ready accomplices (vv. 11-14).—Following instructions, the council summoned the inhabitants of Jezreel to a fast as an acknowledgment of guilt for a so-far unstated offense committed by someone in the community. Naboth was immediately "set . . . on high" as the offender, not as a mark of honor, but to make him the target of false accusation. Two "sons of Belial," worthless men, testified that he had blasphemed against God and the king. It is likely that Naboth had discussed with others his confrontation with Ahab, but the character of those who witnessed against him indicates that their witness was false. Innocent words were distorted to make a case against Naboth, who was condemned and put to death.

III. A Prophet's Denunciation (1 Kings 21:17-24)

According to 2 Kings 9:26, Naboth's sons were slain with him. This appears to have been an arbitrarry act of murder, with little or no legal justification, carried out to ensure that there were no claimants for the coveted vineyard. When the news was given to Ahab that the land was his to take, he asked no questions, but hurried over to claim the property for himself (1 Kings 21:15-16). However great the responsibility that rested on Jezebel, Ahab shared her guilt to the full for his eager acceptance of a situation that was full of ugly probabilities.

17 And the word of the Lord came to Elijah the Tishbite, saying,

18 Arise, go down to meet Ahab king of Israel, which is in Samaria: behold, he is in the vineyard of Naboth, whither he is gone down to possess it.

19 And thus shalt thou speak unto him, saying, Thus saith the Lord, Hast thou killed, and also taken possession? And thou shalt speak unto him, saying, Thus saith the Lord, In the place where dogs licked the blood of Naboth shall dogs lick thy blood, even thine.

1. The prophet Elijah (v. 17).—The last previous reference to Elijah told how he anointed Elisha as his successor (19:19-21). In the next chapter, other prophets are mentioned, but not named. Was Elijah called out of retirement to confront Ahab in the vineyard of Naboth? Whatever the case, this man who had once fled under threat of death from Jezebel mustered his courage, and in the name of God, went to meet the king.

2. Dramatic confrontation (vv. 18-19).—The distance between Samaria, Ahab's capital, and Jezreel, his summer home, was not more than twenty miles. The king apparently received news of Naboth's death while in Samaria, and made a quick journey to take possession of his ill-gotten property. As he was gloating over his acquisition, Elijah suddenly appeared. In a very real sense, the king was caught red-handed. His sentence was suited to his crime. It was fulfilled when Ahab was in battle with the Syrians. He was allied with Jehoshapahat, king of Judah. Ahab was clearly apprehensive, and went into battle disguised. But an enemy archer "drew a bow at a venture," that is, loosed his arrow without a precise target. That arrow struck Ahab so that he died, "and the dogs licked up his blood . . . according unto the word of the Lord" (chap. 22).

3. Serve judgment (vv. 20-24).—Another penalty was pronounced on Ahab, namely, the end of his dynasty. In verses 27-29 we are told how this king, reacting to Elijah's solemn words, "rent his clothes, and put sackcloth upon his flesh, and fasted, and lay in sackcloth, and went softly." These were acts of remorse, if not repentance, and because of them God told Elijah that the second part of the penalty would be postponed. Ahab would pay for his sin by his death, but the royal house would survive him. "I will not bring the evil in his days" (v. 29). God's judgments are often deferred to give opportunity for repentance. He is "not willing that any should perish, but that all should come to repentance" (2 Pet. 3:9). Two sons of Ahab succeeded him, Ahaziah and Jehoram. The first ruled for only two years and was then succeeded by his brother who reigned for twelve. A verdict on his reign says, "He wrought evil in the sight of the Lord; but not like his father, and like his mother" (2 Kings 3:2). The mother, Jezebel, lived throughout his reign and met a gruesome death, as prophesied by

Elijah (9:30-37). With the deaths of these two, mother and son, ended the dynasty of Omri to be succeeded by that of Jehu. Thus, the full penalty of Ahab's sin was met. Jehoram died on the property that had been Naboth's as divine judgment came full circle (9:24-26).

APPLYING THE LESSON

What has changed?—Two friends were talking, one of whom recently was married. The other one asked, "Has your wife changed much?" "Yes," the new husband replied, "She changed my friends, my habits, my diet, my sleeping schedule. . . ." Truth is, we are often changed by our mate, sometimes for the better and sometimes for the worse. Ahab was no saint to start with, although he probably had some good qualities. Evidently, Jezebel brought out the worst in him.

The courage to take a stand.—Jackie Robinson, who broke the color line in baseball, often faced abuse from the fans. He might not have made it without the constant encouragement and help of Pee Wee Reese. When the team was informed that death threats were made against Jackie Robinson who wore number 42, Pee Wee said, "I've got an idea. We'll all wear number 42. They won't know who to shoot at."

It is easy to have convictions when your convictions are not challenged. But when facing a dangerous foe who could easily destroy you, it takes a little more courage.

Elijah was one of the most effective of the Old Testament prophets, not because of the uniqueness of his message but because of the uniqueness of his courage.

Just that adjacent to mine.—A large landowner in Puritan New England was chided for owning so much land. He was often asked, "How much do you intend to buy?" His simple answer was, "Just the land that adjoins mine."

Ahab was motivated by that same spirit. He had much, but much was not enough. He wanted the other land adjoining his.

Handling power alone.—Richard J. Foster has written some probing challenges to the modern world in his books. In *Money, Sex, and Power* he deals with these three forces with which men of every age have had to deal. In one chapter he explains the importance of everyone being accountable to someone. "Nothing," he says, "is more dangerous than leaders accountable to no one." He adds, "Power is just too dangerous a thing for any of us to face alone." He concludes, "If we will look at the abuses of power in the Church today, very often we will see that behind them is someone who has decided that he or she has a direct pipeline to God and therefore does not need the counsel and correction of the community."[2]

Foster directs his challenge toward spiritual leaders. His conclusions apply to any leader, secular or spiritual. Power corrupts, and absolute power corrupts absolutely.

The key to understanding the tragic life of Ahab is to watch how power ultimately corrupted his life.

What courage!—The woman rushed into the dentist's office with her husband. She said, "I need to have a tooth pulled out, and I need you to do it right now. Don't use any Novocain. I don't care about the pain or anything. Just pull it right now because we have to leave town right away. Just pull it out." The dentist said, "I have never met a person like you in all my life. Never have I seen such a courageous person in the dentist's office. Which tooth is it?" She turned to her husband said, "Show him your tooth!"

Most of us can be brave when it is someone else's tooth or someone else's pain. But when the pain or problem is ours, we're not quite as courageous.

Elijah had to take a stand which could jeopardize his own life. Yet, he had the courage to take a stand.

The hurtfulness of sin.—The message of the Bible is summarized in a statement I once heard from an old country preacher. He said, "Sin is not hurtful because God forbids it but rather God forbids it because it is hurtful."

Sin is hurtful to others. Whenever we sin, because our lives are intertwined, other people's lives will be affected.

Sin is hurtful to us. Whenever we sin, we put into motion a series of events which will eventually come back to us. Sin is an action which has consequences. The consequences of sin are damaging to our lives.

Sin is also hurtful to God. It breaks His heart, and it often detours and delays the unfolding of His plan.

We see all these hurtful effects of sin in the experience of Ahab. It hurt Naboth, it hurt God, and it eventually hurt Ahab.

TEACHING THE CLASS

Main Idea: Injustice and corruption incur divine judgment.

Suggested Teaching Aim: Learners will describe the effect on their lives of God's judgment on injustice and corruption.

Introduce the Bible Study

Note that the study for today begins a new unit titled "Counsel and Conflict in the North." Share information from *Studying the Bible* about the division of Israel. State that the unit will deal with the divine judgment of God necessitated by corruption and injustice.

Ask: How frequently do you hear discussion of the judgment of God on persons? Note that God's judgment is not a generally emphasized quality of God.

Draw a vertical line of the chalkboard. On one side write

"God's Love." On the other side write "God's Judgment." Invite learners to suggest words that describe both these qualities of God's character. Write the words on the chalkboard as they are suggested. Suggestions may include the following. God's love—eternal, forgiving, available to all, greater than sin, unconditional. God's judgment—eternal, inescapable, severe, applicable to all persons.

When the two qualities have been contrasted, ask: Why is it more difficult to describe the judgment of God? Note that creates conflict within ourselves and may be hard for us to reconcile with His love. State that the purpose of the study today is to help us to consider the awesomeness of God's judgment and its effect on our own lives.

Search for Biblical Truth

Invite learners to open their Bibles to 1 Kings 21. Share the story "What has changed?" found in *Applying the Lesson*. Remind learners of some of the history that involved Jezebel and Elijah. See *Studying the Bible*.

A Teaching Outline

1. Contrast God's characteristics of life and judgment.
2. Discover an example of God's judgment on injustice and corruption in the Scripture for today.
3. State some principles related to God's judgment.
4. Consider the effect of God's judgment on our behavior.

Call on a learner to read aloud 1 Kings 21:1-4. Share information from *Studying the Bible* about the customs of the day.

Ask: How would you describe Ahab's reaction? Why was he so depressed? Share the story "Just that adjacent to mine" *(Applying the Lesson)*.

Call on a learner to read verses 5-7 aloud from a modern-speech translation to emphasize the quality of the conversation between Ahab and Jezebel. Direct learners to read verses 8-11 to themselves to discover Jezebel's plan for giving Ahab what he wanted. Call for response. Share information about this event from *Studying the Bible*.

Note that at this point Elijah enters the picture. Share information from *Studying the Bible* about Elijah's apparent retirement. Call on a learner to read verses 17-19 aloud. Ask: How do you think Elijah felt when called on to deliver this message to the king? Share stories "The courage to take a stand" and "What courage" *(Applying the Lesson)*.

Give the Truth a Personal Focus

Direct learners to look again at the judgment of God pronounced on Ahab. (v. 19) Ask: Does the judgment seem consistent with the way God's judgment was described as the study was begun? What words need to be added to the list on the chalkboard?

Display the following principles about the judgment of God which are based on this passage.

1. Inability to deal with not having things your way is a step toward embracing injustice.
2. Unwisely releasing control of your authority can create disaster and bring God's judgment.
3. God's judgment will find you, accuse you, and take a severe toll.

Ask rhetorically: Do you believe these principles? What difference would it make in our lives if we really believed them?

---

1. Alfred Edersheim, *Bible History*, Volume 5 (Grand Rapids: Eerdmans, 1940), 178.
2. Richard J. Foster, *Money, Sex, and Power* (San Francisco: Harper and Row, 1985), 240.

September 30

Micaiah and Ahab

Basic Passage: 1 Kings 22:1-40

Focal Passages: 1 Kings 22:13-16,19-23,26-28

The setting of this lesson is still in the reign of Ahab, king of Israel. That country, and the Southern Kingdom of Judah, had enjoyed peace for a number of years (1 Kings 22:1). Relationships between the two kingdoms had improved. One indication of this was the marriage of Athaliah, daughter of Ahab and Jezebel, to the son of Jehoshaphat, king of Judah (2 Kings 8:18). It was natural that this union should bring the two families together. But our chapter would indicate that Ahab had a political purpose in arranging the meeting described in 1 Kings 22:2. Following a defeat of the Syrians by Ahab, Benhadad, their king, had promised to restore all captured cities. One important city, however, Ramoth-gilead, remained in Syrian hands. Situated east of Jordan, Ramoth-gilead was of great strategic value being located on a bluff that provided views of large areas of country. The need to take possession of this city was agreed upon by Jehoshaphat, who, however, had misgivings about the project. In his hesitation, prophetic advice was sought, thus bringing into prominence a man of God, Micaiah, of whom this is the Bible's sole reference.

Study Aim: *To stimulate awareness that not all who claim to speak in the name of God are sincere or truthful*

STUDYING THE BIBLE

Again we need to study the entire background material (1 Kings 22:1-40) in order to understand the subject and draw maximum advantage from it. The story unfolded here is also found in 2 Chronicles 18, with minor differences, including a description of the generous hospitality that Ahab showed to his visitor, Jehoshaphat (v. 2).

I. Prophets True and False (1 Kings 22:1-6)

Whether as a genuine expression of desire to know God's will, or as a concession to religious custom, Jehoshaphat conditioned his agreement to go into battle on obtaining "the word of the Lord" (v. 5). Ahab responded by gathering together four hundred prophets to whom he put the question, "Shall I go against Ramoth-gilead to battle, or shall I forbear?" (v. 6) As one man, they replied that he should go into battle and would win the victory. Jehoshaphat was not impressed. He had reason to suspect the sincerity of a reply so unanimous. Perhaps he knew something of the character of these 400. According to 1 Kings 18:4, Jezebel had attempted to exterminate all "the prophets of the Lord," but at least 100 escaped. Their number may have been increased by men who accepted the fact that survival depended on compromise. In this incident they appear as false prophets who spoke the words the king wanted to hear. Those who make popularity and acceptance their aim, are usually willing to shape their message to the taste of their audience.

II. Call for Micaiah (1 Kings 22:7-18)

Showing great depth of perception, Jehoshaphat wanted to know if there was not one prophet in the Northern Kingdom who could be trusted to speak with integrity. Ahab was compelled to acknowledge that there was one, Micaiah (My-kay-uh). We know nothing of him beyond what is recorded here. Clearly he had prophesied before at the request of Ahab, but would not adapt his message to please the king's ear. He spoke truth, even when it hurt. As a result, Ahab said, "I hate him; for he doth not prophesy good concerning me, but evil" (v. 8). Royal hatred had apparently led to the abuse of Micaiah, for an officer was sent to get him, presumably from prison, where he was later returned. An example of a false prophet is furnished in Zedekiah (v. 11), whose name meant "God is my righteousness." He was false in name as well as in message. Adapting a common practice among Old Testament prophets, that is, dramatizing what he had to say, Zedekiah made "horns of iron" as symbols of the brute strength with which he claimed that Ahab would defeat his enemy.

13 And the messenger that was gone to call Micaiah spake unto him, saying, Behold now, the words of the prophets declare good unto the king with one mouth: let thy word, I pray thee, be like the word of one of them, and speak that which is good.

14 And Micaiah said, As the Lord liveth, what the Lord saith unto me, that will I speak.

15 So he came to the king. And the king said unto him, Micaiah, shall we go against Ramoth-gilead to battle, or shall we forbear? And he answered him, Go, and prosper: for the Lord shall deliver it into the hand of the king.

16 And the king said unto him, How many times shall I adjure thee that thou tell me nothing but that which is true in the name of the Lord?

The world cannot understand why, in the interests of truth and integrity, a person would go against the tide at personal risk. Hence the advice given to Micaiah to join the four hundred in telling Ahab what he wanted to hear. This was the path of prudence that any person in his right mind would take. But Micaiah would have none of this. He would speak only "what the Lord saith unto me." This is the spirit of the true prophet already exemplified for us in Samuel, Nathan, and Elijah, men who were prepared to hazard their lives in order to be faithful messengers for God. Why, then, in his first statement to Ahab, did Micaiah side with the false prophets (v. 15)? Had we been present to hear the tone of Micaiah's voice, and seen the expression on his face, we would doubtless have detected irony. It was as though he said to the king, "If this is what you want to hear, this is what I will say." Ahab was not deceived for this prophet had never before been a yes man. He insisted that Micaiah speak what was on his mind. But Ahab's insistence was an empty gesture for he would reject advice, however given, that was contrary to his wishes. Ahab got the truth in a vivid figure of a flock of sheep, scattered and without a shepherd (v. 17).

III. The Truth Rejected (1 Kings 22:19-28)

Ahab understood Micaiah's statement about shepherd and sheep. The idea of the king as shepherd to his people is frequent in the Old Testament. Therefore, sheep without a master (v. 17) signified a nation without its king. If Ahab decided to go into battle against the Syrians, this would cost him his life. But in the petulant mood, Ahab said to Jehoshaphat, "Did I not tell thee that he would prophesy no good concerning me, but evil?" (v. 18) The prophet's advice had been rejected in advance. But Micaiah had not said his last word. He proceeded to tell the king why the false prophets had spoken as they did. They were possessed of "a lying spirit" (v. 22).

19 And he said, Hear thou therefore the word of the Lord: I saw the Lord sitting on his throne, and all the host of heaven standing by him on his right hand and on his left.

20 And the Lord said, Who shall persuade Ahab, that he may go up and fall at Ramoth-gilead? And one said on this manner, and another said on that manner.

21 And there came forth a spirit, and stood before the Lord and said, I will persuade him.

22 And the Lord said unto him, Wherewith? And he said, I will go forth, and I will be a lying spirit in the mouth of all his prophets. And he said, Thou shalt persuade him, and prevail also: go forth, and do so.

23 Now therefore, behold, the Lord hath put a lying spirit in the mouth of all these thy prophets, and the Lord hath spoken evil concerning thee.

We must go back to 21:19 where Elijah, speaking in God's name, foretold the violent death of Ahab. How would this come to pass? Micaiah's explanation was that God permitted a lying spirit to take possession of Ahab's favorite prophets so that they would recommend a course that would lead to his death. In early Hebrew theology, God's sovereignty was absolute. Everything that happened was according to His will, or with His permission.

This did not mean that Ahab was under coercion to follow the advice of the false prophets. The decision was his and the consequences his to bear. Micaiah's explanation did not sit well with Zedekiah, the false prophet who had made the "horns of iron" (v. 11). He struck Micaiah in anger, and the king ordered him to be returned to prison. Such is the price of telling the truth when people prefer to listen to lies.

26 And the king of Israel said, Take Micaiah, and carry him back unto Amon the governor of the city, and to Joash the king's son:

27 And say, Thus saith the king, Put this fellow in the prison, and feed him with bread of affliction and with water of afflicition, until I come in peace.

28 And Micaiah said, If thou return at all in peace, the Lord hath not spoken by men. And he said, Hearken, O people, everyone of you.

In defiance of the prophet and his words, Ahab put Micaiah back in prison, and on prison diet, "until I come in peace." What he had in mind to do to the prophet, had he returned in peace, we can only conjecture. But this good man was not to be silenced by the prospect of prison. He was prepared to let the fate of Ahab be the test of his veracity. This must always be the test of prophetic words, either they come to pass, or they do not. So sure was Micaiah that he was the messenger of the Lord that, as they dragged him away, he said to the watching crowds, "Hearken, O people, every one of you." Nothing is said about the reaction of Jehoshaphat. Apparently he had so compromised himself that he had no choice but to go along with the suicidal course chosen by Ahab. The tragedy of a descendant of David allied with a semi-pagan king needs little comment.

IV. The Inevitable Consequence (1 Kings 22:29-37)

Ahab's obstinacy was mixed with a heavy dose of fear. He would go into battle against the Syrians, but take precautions to save his life. He persuaded Jehoshaphat to wear his customary battle dress, while he put on a disguise. At one point, the king of Judah was mistaken for Ahab and the Syrians pressed the attack. But that king let his identity be known, and escaped to safety. Ahab probably congratulated himself on the success of his disguise. But he could not escape the judgment pronounced against him. Although the king of Syria had told his men to focus their attack on Ahab (v. 31), it was a stray arrow that penetrated his armor and killed him. He was carried dying from the field of battle, and as the news of his mortal wounding became known, the cry went up among his followers, "Every man to his city, and every man to his own country" (v. 36). Like sheep without a shepherd, as Micaiah had prophesied, his army broke up, and every soldier went his own way. The words of God's true prophets, Elijah and Micaiah, had come to fulfillment. Surely the next generation would learn its lesson. But see verses 51-53.

APPLYING THE LESSON

Doing the will of God.—One of the true saints of the ages was Saint Francis of Assisi. Born to an affluent family, he forsook all of his material abundance and gave his life in service and ministry to the poor. He travelled throughout the countryside with nothing, living in total trust on the Lord. He believed this was God's will for his life.

How did Saint Francis realize this was God's will for him? According to one story, he sat down with his Gospel and made the sign of the cross over it. Then, he opened it to three places, reading the three texts. The first was the story of the rich young man who refused to sell his goods and went away from the Lord sorrowfully. The second was the commandment to the disciples to take nothing with them on their journey, neither money nor staff. The third was the saying that the disciple of Jesus must take up his cross daily and follow Him. These three passages became the guidelines for Francis and his followers, for he interpreted them as God's will for his life.

However you discover it, every Christian should follow God's will for his life. Jehoshaphat apparently wanted to know if it was God's will for him to join with Ahab in the campaign against Benhadad.

Telling the truth.—The lawyer was badgering the witness at the trial. To intimidate the witness even further, the attorney said, "You seem to have plenty of intelligence for a man in your position." The witness responded, "Thank you. If I weren't under oath, I'd return the compliment."

Dishonesty is such a part of life today it is difficult to know if a person is telling the truth, even if they are under oath. It is not a new problem. Jehoshaphat had reason to question the honesty of the 400 prophets of Ahab. They all said the same thing, but Jehoshaphat wasn't sure they were telling the truth.

I would rather be right.—Henry Clay was a perennial candidate for President of the United States, a position he very much wanted but never obtained. On one occasion, when Henry Clay took an unpopular position on a particular issue, his adviser said, "Mr. Clay, if you take that position, you will never be elected President of the United States." Henry Clay responded, "I would rather be right than be President."

That is integrity, standing up for what is right instead of what is convenient. We see another demonstration of such integrity in the life of Micaiah.

Dealing with enemies.—Two English schoolboys took a dislike to each other and the hatred grew more intense as the years passed. One entered the Royal Navy and became an admiral. The other went into church work and eventually became a bishop. They met years later, the bishop, who had become very plump, dressed in his robe, and the admiral, who had become very gray, dressed in his uniform. However, they immediately recognized each other and the years of hatred came boiling to the surface. The bishop said, "Stationmaster, from which platform does the 10:05 train leave for Oxford?" The admiral responded, without batting an eye, "Platform five, madam. But in your condition, should you be traveling?"

Zedekiah had that some feeling of hatred toward Micaiah, and we see it manifested in the lesson.

Didn't put my full weight down.—Joan was 70 years old and had never flown on a plane. She really had no intention of flying on a plane. However, grandchildren motivate you to do things you wouldn't ordinarily do. Because her grandchildren were growing up 1,000 miles away, she decided the only way to see them was to fly to their home. Reluctantly, she boarded the plane and made the flight. When her children greeted her at the airport, they asked her how she liked her flight. "Oh," he said, "it was all right. But I never did put my full weight down."

Sometimes our fear is unwarranted. At other times, we have a reason to be afraid. Ahab's fear was of this latter kind. He knew that Micaiah's prophecy was from God, so when Micaiah said he had a vision that Ahab would be killed in the battle, Ahab was justifiably afraid. His attempt to fight under disguise was a result of his fear.

TEACHING THE LESSON

Main Idea: All who speak in the name of God are not sincere and truthful.

Suggested Teaching Aim: Learners will state guidelines for determining whether a message given by another is true.

Introduce the Bible Study

Ask: Do you believe everything you hear? Why or why not? Continue: Do you believe everything that you hear a preacher or Bible teacher say? Why or why not? After a brief response, ask: How do you decide whether the speaker is giving God's truth? Note that the guideline of whether it is what the Bible says does not provide a complete solution since much interpretation of the Scripture is needed. Ask: Whose interpretation do you believe?

Note that this issue is the bottom line for the study today. State that the purpose of the study is for learners to develop some guidelines that will help them determine whether a message given by another person is truly from God.

Search for Biblical Truth

Invite learners to open their Bibles to 1 Kings 22. Call on a learner who has previously agreed to tell this event to the class and has studied the entire background material in preparation. Have the story told before the Scripture is read to prepare the learners for understanding the focal passage. When the incidents have been described, call on three other learners who have previously agreed to read the focal passage aloud. Reader 1: verses 13-16. Reader 2: verses 19-23. Reader 3: verses 26-28. When the reading is finished, share information about Ahab's death found in *Studying the Bible*.

Remind learners that the purpose of today's study is to learn some ways that we can use to validate a message that is said to be from God. Direct them to work with those sitting near them to identify some principles that grow out of this passage of Scripture about those who claim to speak the message of God. After several minutes of discussion, call for response. Responses should include ideas similar to the following.

A Teaching Outline

1. Consider the question: Who do you believe?
2. Discover an example of untruthful and unreliable persons claiming to speak for God.
3. Identify some guidelines for determining whether to accept that a messenger is speaking God's message.
4. Make the guidelines useful in personal situations.

1. There is pressure for God's messengers to speak what others want to hear (vv. 13-14). Share "Telling the truth" *(Applying the Lesson)*.

2. Wisdom indicates that you should consider how the message is given as well as what the message is (vv. 15-16). Share "Doing the will of God" *(Applying the Lesson)*.

3. Some who claim to speak for God are telling lies (vv. 19-23).

4. Popularity and prosperity are not an indication of the hand of God upon a messenger (vv. 26-27). Share "I would rather be right" *(Applying the Lesson)*.

5. The outcome is the ultimate measure of the validity of a message said to be from God (v. 28). Share "Didn't put my full weight down" *(Applying the Lesson)*.

Give the Truth a Personal Focus

Ask: Based on these principles, what are some questions we might ask to guide us in determining whether a message is truly from God? Elicit response from learners. Response should include the following questions. What pressures might be on the messenger to speak the message he is giving? Is the speaker speaking facetiously or resolutely? Am I believing his message because he is popular or prosperous? Am I taking into account that some who claim to be messengers of God are deceivers and liars? Is the messenger willing to validate his message by staying around to see the outcome?

Writers

Studying the Bible

Donald F. Ackland has written this portion of *Broadman Comments* since 1970. For over sixty years he has ministered the Word of God by tongue and pen. He is a popular Bible conference leader, has authored several books, and is a Sunday School teacher in his home church.

Applying the Lesson

Brian L. Harbour is pastor, Immanuel Baptist Church, Little Rock, Arkansas. He is the author of many books and is popular as a preacher at numerous conferences.

Teaching the Class

Polly Cooper is a psychologist, The Counseling and Development Center, First Baptist Church, Dallas, Texas. She has been writing teaching procedures for adults since 1972.